Paul Duncan

STANLEY KUBRICK

Visual Poet 1928–1999

TASCHEN

KÖLN LONDON LOS ANGELES MADRID PARIS TOKYO

FRONT COVER
Still from '2001: A Space Odyssey' (1968)
Bowman beholds the wonders of the universe.

FIRST PAGE
Stanley Kubrick
Examining film of 'The Shining' (1980).

FRONTISPIECE
Stanley Kubrick
On the set of 'Spartacus' (1960).

THIS PAGE
1 **On the set of 'Dr Strangelove' (1964)** Stanley Kubrick lines up a shot in his viewfinder.
2 **On the set of '2001: A Space Odyssey' (1968)** Kubrick on the Moon excavation set.
3 **On the set of 'A Clockwork Orange' (1971)** Stanley Kubrick films Mr Alexander (Patrick Magee) being gagged.

OPPOSITE
1 **On the set of 'Barry Lyndon' (1975)**
2 **On the set of 'Eyes Wide Shut' (1999)** Stanley Kubrick gathers Tom Cruise, Nicole Kidman and Sydney Pollack around a television to see a video playback of their scene together.

PAGES 6/7
On the set of 'Spartacus' (1960)
Stanley Kubrick stands behind the camera as Woody Strode and Kirk Douglas fight.

BACK COVER
Stanley Kubrick
Photo by Christiane Kubrick.

© 2003 TASCHEN GmbH
Hohenzollernring 53, D–50672 Köln
www.taschen.com
Editor/Layout: Paul Duncan/Wordsmith Solutions
Typeface Design: Sense/Net, Andy Disl, Cologne

Printed in Italy
ISBN 3–8228–1592–6

Notes

A superscript number indicates a reference to a note on page 192

Images

British Film Institute Stills, Posters and Designs, London: Front
    Cover, 4(3), 8, 10, 11, 12left, 25, 31, 32, 34/35, 36, 38, 47,
    48, 50, 52top, 53t, 57t, 58, 60right, 61r, 76 (2), 77left, 78/79,
    80 (2), 81 (2), 82, 86r, 88, 89, 90, 91, 92 (2), 93 (2), 94 (2),
    95 (2), 96, 97, 98 (4), 99, 101, 104 (2), 108/109, 110bottom,
    111 (2), 113, 114, 115, 116, 117, 120/121, 124, 125, 128t,
    129, 130/131, 132, 135, 136 (2), 138/139, 142, 143, 144,
    146 (2), 147 (2), 150, 151, 152b, 156, 157, 163, 169t, 171b,
    178, 182, 186, 188 (3), 190r
PWE Verlag / defd-movies, Hamburg: 1, 5 (2), 12r, 13, 24, 39,
    40/41, 42, 43 (2), 44/45, 46, 49, 51t, 52b, 53b, 56t, 61l, 62,
    68, 69, 74/75, 77r, 86l, 87r, 100, 107, 110t, 112, 118/119,
    126/127, 128b, 133, 158, 159, 160, 164/165, 167, 168,
    169b, 171t, 174 (2), 175, 176/177, 180, 181, 183, 187, 189tl,
    191bl + b centre + r, Back Cover
Herbert Klemens / Filmbild Fundus Robert Fischer, Munich: 30,
    33, 51b, 56b, 57b, 60l, 87l, 148/149, 152t, 154, 155 (2), 161,
    162, 170, 185
The Kobal Collection, London/New York: 6/7, 54, 55, 72, 83,
    84/85, 102/103, 106, 122/123, 134, 140/141, 172/173
ICCARUS, Munich and Library of Congress, Washington: 16, 17,
    18, 19, 20, 21, 22, 23
J.R. Eyerman/Timepix, New York: 63, 64/65, 70/71
Richard C. Miller/MPTV, Los Angeles: 2, 66/67
Courtesy of the Kubrick Estate: 29

Copyright

Prelude

Early in his life Stanley Kubrick realised: "We are capable of the greatest good and the greatest evil, and the problem is that we often can't distinguish between them when it suits our purpose."[1] This was one of his major themes, a riff he played in all of his films. Good and evil. Love and hate. Sex and violence. Desire and fear. Fidelity and betrayal. Each of the central characters in his movies wrestled with these forces within them, and their external circumstances (a war, an affair, a crime) helped to focus that struggle for the benefit of the audience.

Kubrick reiterated this idea when he talked about his horror movie *The Shining*: "There's something inherently wrong with the human personality. There's an evil side to it. One of the things that horror stories can do is to show us the archetypes of the unconscious; we can see the dark side without having to confront it directly."[2] In his biography of Kubrick, John Baxter wrote that this attitude towards the story and characters can be applied to all of Kubrick's films – it is a Manichaean view of the universe which says that the world is not created by God but by the powers of good and evil wrestling for control. For example, in Kubrick's first film, *Fear and Desire*, the 'good' soldiers who crash behind enemy lines confront and kill the 'bad' soldiers who were played by the same actors. In *A Clockwork Orange*, Alex may be a brutal, thuggish adolescent who loves sex and violence, but he also loves the *Ninth Symphony* of Ludwig Van Beethoven. At the end of the story, Alex's uncontrollable vices are returned to him, but so too is his love of the *Ninth Symphony*. The plot of *Full Metal Jacket*, in some ways a reworking of *Fear and Desire*, can be seen as Joker's Odyssey to find his evil self – he may be a sensitive writer, an intellectual, but occasionally he has to find and unleash the animal inside him. As they said in Vietnam, "Yea, though I walk through the valley of the Shadow of Death, I will fear no Evil, for I *am* the Evil." Kubrick showed this dichotomy on the *Full Metal Jacket* poster in which a soldier's helmet has both a peace symbol and the words 'Born To Kill' on it.

With each of Kubrick's films, the inner struggle is examined from a different perspective. Sometimes it is seen from the point of view of a character whose nature comes into conflict with society, as is the case with Alex in *A Clockwork Orange* and Humbert Humbert in *Lolita*. In other films, the characters' experiences or training make them act the way they do, as with Redmond Barry in

On the set of 'A Clockwork Orange' (1971)
Stanley Kubrick (foreground) watches the droogs beat up the old drunk.

"Anyone who has ever been privileged to direct a film knows that, although it can be like trying to write War and Peace *in a bumper car at an amusement park, when you finally get it right, there are not many joys in life that can equal the feeling."*

Stanley Kubrick [30]

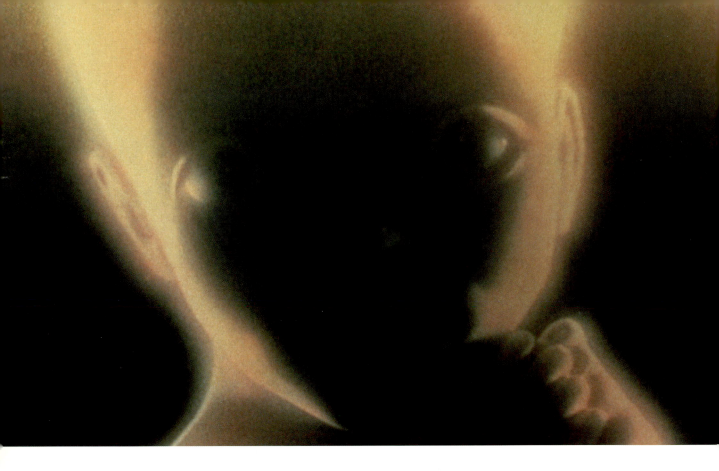

Barry Lyndon and Dr Bill Harford in *Eyes Wide Shut*. In many cases, the duality within the character is shown through the symbolism of mirrors, or through the actions of other people in the narrative. Humbert dares not profess his love for Lolita, but his hidden dark side in the form of Clare Quilty has no such inhibitions and makes love to Lolita. Jung called this dark side the Shadow – Kubrick knew Jung's work and quoted it. When Dr Bill Harford is told by his wife that she almost gave up their marriage on a sudden desire for a stranger, he is shaken but not convinced. He is then called away and a woman he hardly knows declares her love for him. Her fiancé enters and looks just like Bill – the couple are a mirror image of Bill and his wife. Having experienced this, Dr Bill is now convinced and for the rest of the movie he examines his Shadow.

After establishing the struggle within his central character, Kubrick then gave the character two choices, one representing good and the other evil. In *Paths of Glory* Colonel Dax must decide whether to become a bureaucratic general or a lumpen soldier. The trial of the deserters shows us that Dax is repulsed by both options and, in the end, decides to tread his own path. In the beautifully chilling *Barry Lyndon*, our hero rejects love and decides to acquire money and social standing. The outcome, as in all of Kubrick's films, is unpredictable but satisfying. Whether consciously or unconsciously, Kubrick examined the duality and contradictions that exist in all of us.

Critic David Denby once compared Kubrick to the monolith from his film *2001: A Space Odyssey*, calling him 'a force of supernatural intelligence, appearing at great intervals amid high-pitched shrieks, who gives the world a violent kick

Still from 'A Clockwork Orange' (1971)
The malevolence of Alex. It is his nature to be evil.

up the next rung of the evolutionary ladder.' Stanley Kubrick refined this approach to film-making over almost five decades. He presented viewers with a film that met all the marketing and pyrotechnic requirements of films (a genre film, with action, in an exotic setting), but he also gave great thought to the sub-text so that the viewer could discover their own meanings if they so desired. Although film is a mass-market form of entertainment, it can also be an artform and Kubrick made films that would appeal to every sort of viewer, whatever their expectation of film. Kubrick directed four war films, two crime films, two science-fiction films, two historical epics, a horror film and two films about sexual relationships. In an interview with Colin Young, Kubrick explained why he used genre films: "One of the attractions of a war or crime story is that it provides an almost unique opportunity to contrast an individual or our contemporary society with a solid framework of accepted value, which the audience becomes fully aware of, and which can be used as a counterpoint to a human, individual, emotional situation. Further, war acts as a kind of hothouse for forced, quick breeding of attitudes and feelings. Attitudes crystallise and come out into the open. Conflict is natural, when it would in a less critical situation have to be introduced almost as a contrivance, and would thus appear forced or, even worse, false."[3]

The meaning of a film is usually conveyed to an audience through the words of a film reviewer in a newspaper, magazine or book. This analysis is an intellectual exercise that tries to interpret the emotions the reviewer felt whilst watching the film. However, just as each novel has a meaning unique to each reader, so does each film. Consequently, there are as many meanings as there are viewers.

ABOVE
Still from 'Lolita' (1962)
Humbert (James Mason) is intent on killing his
dark half, Clare Quilty (Peter Sellers).

RIGHT
Still from 'Killer's Kiss' (1955)
Davy (Jamie Smith) holds Vincent (Frank Silvera)
at gunpoint in an attempt to rescue Gloria, the
object of their desire.

Kubrick was very careful not to present his own views of the meaning of his films, as he explained to Robert Emmett Ginna in 1960: "One of the things that I always find extremely difficult, when a picture's finished, is when a writer or a film reviewer asks, 'Now, what is it that you were trying to say in that picture?' And without being thought too presumptuous for using this analogy, I like to remember what T. S. Eliot said to someone who had asked him – I believe it was about *The Waste Land* – what he meant by the poem. He replied, 'I meant what it said.' If I could have said it any differently, I would have."[4]

This leads to one conclusion: if you want to understand a Kubrick film you must experience it for yourself. This is easy to do because a Kubrick film is primarily made with a series of images and sounds that combine to elicit an emotional response. We are all capable of doing this, as Kubrick told Joseph Gelmis: "…an Alabama truck driver, whose views in every other respect would be extremely narrow, is able to listen to a Beatles record on the same level of appreciation and perception as a young Cambridge intellectual, because their emotions and subconscious are far more similar than their intellects. The common bond is their subconscious emotional reaction; and I think that a film which can communicate on this level can have a more profound spectrum of impact than any form of traditional verbal communication."[5] This explains why many of Kubrick's films do not have dialogue for long periods and why the story is primarily conveyed through images and music/sound.

It is interesting to note that when the characters do speak, the words emphasise the characters' relationship to their environment and bind them together, like the swearing and jargon of the soldiers in *Full Metal Jacket*, the evocative euphemisms of *Dr Strangelove*, or Nadsat, the adolescent street language invented by Anthony Burgess for his novel *A Clockwork Orange*. As Gilbert Adair wrote in a review of *Full Metal Jacket*: 'Kubrick's approach to language has always been of a reductive and uncompromisingly deterministic nature. He appears to view it as the exclusive product of environmental conditioning, only very marginally influ-

Still from 'Full Metal Jacket' (1987)
Private Joker (Matthew Modine) on patrol in
"a world of shit." He has been trained to kill, but
will he be able to live with himself afterwards?

enced by concepts of subjectivity and interiority, by all the whims, shades and modulations of personal expression.'

Many reviewers have failed to understand that Kubrick's approach to film was non-verbal and often reprimanded him for it. Interestingly, the books about his films that Kubrick collaborated on (by Alexander Walker and Michel Ciment) were primarily interested in the visual storytelling and symbolism of his work. It is my belief that Kubrick was a visual poet whose work was not fully appreciated at the time it was released because many film reviewers did not review it as a visual art form.

Although the visual arts can elicit immediate emotional responses from the viewer, it is only after some contemplation that a fuller and more reasoned understanding can be achieved. Gene D. Phillips observed in his introduction to *Stanley Kubrick Interviews*: 'Early notices, written for newspapers and weekly magazines with immediate deadlines to meet, tended to judge *2001* more harshly than the reviews composed by critics for monthly magazines, who had more time to reflect on the picture.'[6] Kubrick explained further to *Time* magazine in 1975: "The essence of dramatic form is to let an idea come over people without it being plainly stated. When you say something directly, it is simply not as potent as it is when you allow people to discover it for themselves."[7]

"One of the things that gave me the most confidence in trying to make a film was seeing all the lousy films that I saw. Because I sat there and thought: Well, I don't know a goddamn thing about movies, but I know I can make a film better than that."

Stanley Kubrick[4]

How Stanley Kubrick became a film director

On 26 July 1928, Jacques L. Kubrick and his wife Gertrude were proud to announce the birth of their son Stanley at Manhattan's Lying-In Hospital. They returned home to 2160 Clinton Avenue in the Bronx, New York, where the recently-graduated Dr Jacques was working to build up his general practitioner's medicinal practice. Six years later, on 21 May 1934, Stanley had a little sister called Barbara Mary to play with. In September of 1934, Stanley began to attend school or, more precisely, he attended school some of the time. The reason for his continued absences from school over the next few years is unclear, but it is known that he had home tutoring at one stage, that his school stated he lacked social skills and that his reading and writing skills were tested above average. If Stanley was an intelligent child who lacked stimulation, then it was apparent that he needed to be stimulated as soon as possible. Perhaps realising his son's situation, Jacques gave Stanley a Graflex professional camera on his thirteenth birthday. Jacques also gave his son an appreciation of literature and taught him how to play chess. Stanley avidly pursued all three activities for the rest of his life.

In his early teens, Stanley became friendly with a neighbour his own age, Marvin Traub, who was also bitten by the photography bug. Marvin had his own darkroom and, after creating photographic assignments for themselves, both boys spent many hours watching the chemicals magically make images on the photographic paper. Like their photojournalist hero Arthur Fellig (the crime photographer more commonly known as Weegee), they played with and manipulated the images they had captured. Although Stanley sometimes attended William Howard Taft High School and occasionally signed up for other pursuits – he played the drums in a swing band – it was clear to everybody there that this loner was only interested in one thing: photography.

As well as being a member of the school's photography club, which allowed him to cover school and outside events for the school's glossy magazine, Stanley also watched films, any films, at the local cinemas to see how they were shot. Single-minded in his pursuit, Stanley haunted the streets, looking for subjects, catching people unawares, developing his eye for a photo. It was on one of these patrols that Stanley saw a dejected news vendor surrounded by headlines announcing the death of the much-beloved President Franklin Delano Roosevelt.

On the set of 'Fear and Desire' (1953)
Kubrick (right of camera) with his cast (front row), transport (middle row) and crew (back row). He is with his first wife, Toba Metz.

"The best education in film is to make one."
Stanley Kubrick [5]

'Chicago – City of Extremes' (2 April 1949)
Photo essay in 'Look' magazine. Photo by Stanley
Kubrick. From the beginning, Kubrick had the
ability to capture the atmosphere of a place.

**'Working Debutante – Betsy von Furstenberg'
(18 July 1950)**
Photo essay in 'Look' magazine. Photo by
Stanley Kubrick. Note the way that the painting
('Blue Portrait of Angel F. de Soto' (1903) by
Pablo Picasso) ironically comments on the
people in the foreground.

Stanley took the photo to Helen O'Brian, head of the photographic department at *Look*, a glossy photo-dependent magazine that was a competitor to *Life*. She took one look at the photo, immediately recognised its power and purchased it without hesitation for $25. It was printed on 26 June 1945. Stanley was sixteen.

Six months later, Stanley graduated from high school, was made a fully-fledged staff photographer at *Look* and was shown the ropes by the older professionals. He was given every kind of assignment going, whether it was to shoot what an ape saw when it looked out of its cage, or the different emotions experienced by people waiting at the dentist, or to spend time with film stars like Montgomery Clift and get candid shots. During his years at *Look*, Stanley developed his storytelling technique through mini photo stories. One of his first was 'A Short Short in a Movie Balcony' (published 16 April 1946), which is a series of four candid pictures purporting to be of a young man in a cinema making advances on the young woman beside him. He is rebuked for his impertinence. It was a set up – the cinema was closed, the man and woman were Stan's friends and the cinema audience consisted of his younger sister Barbara. Stanley had taken each of his friends aside and given them directions privately. He told the woman to really let the guy have it. So, when the man gets a slap in the face both the slap and his shock reaction are for real. Stanley already knew how to get what he wanted for the camera.

Over the next four years Stanley matured into a photojournalist with a deft eye for composition, atmosphere and timing. One of his earliest photo essays was 'Prizefighter' (published 18 January 1949), which covered the life of middleweight boxer Walter Cartier between two fights. Cartier loses the first fight because of a nasty cut from a head-butt by Tony D'Amico. In the second fight, Cartier knocks out Jimmy Mangia in the first round. Cartier's time between the fights is ordinary and stately, but the fight is fast and vicious.

A long-time lover of boxing, Stanley understood his subject and interpreted it for his audience. Consequently, the day is light, full of laughter, Cartier talking with his family and friends, praying in church and repairing his nephew's toy boat. The camera is static, just looking at the people and finding interest within the frame of the photo. However, the night scenes are dramatic, taken from unusual angles, the solid black punctured with white highlights. Stanley took all twelve pictures for 'What's Your Idea of a Good Time?' (published 10 December 1946). Two pictures featured people he knew. One was Marvin Traub, Stan's former darkroom buddy, who was now a sailor more interested in letting off steam than in waiting for photos to develop. Another photo featured Stan's long-time girlfriend Toba Metz. Their families lived in the same apartment block on Shakespeare Avenue and Toba also went to Taft High School. She liked drawing caricatures of her friends and watching their reactions, she told the magazine. Stanley and Toba's romance blossomed into marriage on 29 May 1948, after which they moved to Greenwich Village. It was obvious to everybody that Stanley was interested in more than just photographs – he was also a film buff. He watched movies all the time, no matter how good or bad. One friend, David Vaughn, said that Kubrick would watch a movie when it was silent, to see how the story was told, and then go back to reading his paper when people started talking. He taught himself how movies were made by reading film theory books and filling them with notes. He fell in love with Prokofiev's music for Sergei

ABOVE
'Prizefighter' (18 January 1949)
Photo essay in 'Look' magazine. Photo by Stanley Kubrick. Walter Cartier waits for his fight to begin.

OPPOSITE
'Prizefighter' (18 January 1949)
Photo essay in 'Look' magazine. Photo by Stanley Kubrick. The fight.

'Columbia – Its New Head is Eisenhower'
(11 May 1948)
Photo essay in 'Look' magazine. Photo by
Stanley Kubrick. '2001: A Space Odyssey' was
the apogee of Kubrick's thinking about man and
science. This photo marries science with
religion.

**'Midsummer Nights in New York'
(26 November 1946)**
Photo essay in 'Look' magazine. Photo by
Stanley Kubrick. Kubrick's interest
in performance meant that he often used
performances in his films to distil his films'
themes.

'N.Y. World Art Center' (8 June 1948)
Photo essay in 'Look' magazine. Photo by
Stanley Kubrick. German artist George Grosz,
who was hated by the Nazis, lived in America
from 1933 to 1959.

Eisenstein's film *Alexander Nevsky*, so he bought the record and played it continuously until his sister Barbara broke it in anger. Some of his colleagues at *Look* had experience of Hollywood, and were happy to answer his questions, but they could not see how a quiet boy like Stanley could ever command big film crews on a set. However, as Alexander Walker explained in *Stanley and Us*, although at that time Stanley was so timid that he would press himself up against a wall to get out of the way of people coming towards him in a corridor, once he was behind a camera he became a different person – he was in control of the world.

Stanley shared a love of film with his friend Alexander Singer – they had both been encouraged by their high school art teacher Herman Getter to investigate and use movie cameras. When Alex graduated from high school, he read and adapted Homer's *The Iliad* with the intention of directing it for a major studio. When it became evident that this was perhaps a little too ambitious, he wrote, scripted and drew storyboards for a short love story. He showed them to Stanley on top of a double-decker bus going down Fifth Avenue. Up until that point Stanley wanted to become a cinematographer but, after seeing the storyboards, Stanley realised that the crucial part of film-making was making the decision about what to film. From that moment on, Stanley wanted to direct as well as photograph and edit his own films.

Stanley began his career as an independent film-maker when he made *Day of the Fight* in 1950. He had learned through Alex Singer, who worked as an office boy at Time Inc. where the newsreel *The March of Time* was made, that it cost $40,000 to make each short film. Stanley could not afford that much money, but he did have $1,500 savings to make a similar short film and to sell it independently. Deciding to revisit his work on his 'Prizefighter' photo essay, Kubrick contacted the Cartier twins (Vincent Cartier was Walter's manager) and quickly gained their co-operation. He spent time with them, followed their daily routine and then filmed it. In Vincent LoBrutto's biography, *Stanley Kubrick*, Vincent Cartier commented: "Stanley was a very stoic, impassive but imaginative type person with strong, imaginative thoughts. He commanded respect in a quiet, shy way. Whatever he wanted, you complied, he just captivated you. Anybody who worked with Stanley did just what Stanley wanted."[8]

The structure of the film follows that of the photo essay. Fighter Walter Cartier and lawyer/manager Vincent wake up, go to church and have communion, then cook breakfast. Walter goes for a check-up, to make sure he is fit and the right weight for the fight, then he eats at his favourite diner, the Steak Joint on Greenwich Avenue. At home, Walter plays with his dog. (In fact, it wasn't his dog. Kubrick introduced the dog to add 'human interest' as his journalist friends called it.) Preparing to leave, Walter looks at himself in the mirror and presses his nose down to see what it looks like when broken. At the stadium, Walter prepares himself in a small room and is called into the ring. In the ensuing fight, Walter knocks out Bobby James. It is just another day in the life of a boxer.

Day of the Fight is remarkably accomplished for a first film. As well as the superb photography and framing, there are stylistic touches that show, in retrospect, that Kubrick had emerged fully formed as a film-maker. There is a narrator who gives us useful information. Kubrick used a voice-over in many of his films for differing effects. For example, *A Clockwork Orange* is narrated by a charis-

"I don't think that writers or painters or film-makers function because they have something they particularly want to say. They have something that they feel."

Stanley Kubrick[24]

'Montgomery Clift – Glamor Boy in Baggy Pants' (19 July 1949)
Photo essay in 'Look' magazine. Photo by Stanley Kubrick.

matic thug and *Barry Lyndon* is punctuated by the sarcastic tones of Michael Hordern. There is a sequence in *Day of the Fight* where the Cartier twins walk towards us and the camera moves backwards. This reverse tracking shot, as it is known, is one of Kubrick's most recognisable camera movements and is used in every movie. It implies that the walker is thrusting, dynamic, decisive, in control and powerful. During the fight between Cartier and Bobby James, Kubrick threw his hand into the ring and filmed the punching from the point of view of the canvas. In contrast to the controlled, stately shots that are associated with him, Kubrick often used his journalistic training to shoot blind or to get opportunistic shots from unusual angles. The hand-held camera gives a sense of immediacy and veracity to the image. When the shoot was finished, Kubrick cut the film together and added a score by Singer's friend Gerald Fried. Kubrick had spent $3,900 to make the film, and he sold it to RKO-Pathé for $4,000, the most they had ever paid for a short film. Although the profit margin was only $100, Kubrick took the money because RKO had also advanced him $1,500 for his next short film.

Flying Padre is a slick, professional piece of work about the Reverend Fred Stadtmueller who, the voice-over tells us, travels by plane because his eleven churches are situated in four thousand square miles of territory. Over the course of two days Stadtmueller performs a burial service, flies back home to deliver a mass, sorts out a boy bullying a little girl, then makes an emergency flight to get a sick mother and baby to an ambulance.

This film was like many of the assignments that Kubrick had been asked to do at *Look* – an unusual human-interest story. However, Kubrick manages to sneak a few of his own touches into the eight minutes. There are many views of the airplane, and from the airplane, that are later echoed in the almost fetishistic depiction of spacecraft in *2001: A Space Odyssey*. The close-ups of faces at the funeral are reminiscent of the style of Sergei Eisenstein, the Russian director of *Battleship Potemkin* (1925) and *Ivan the Terrible* (1942), whose work Kubrick studied intensely at this time. Kubrick leaves the best shot until last, when the ambulance speeds away from the Reverend standing in front of his plane. It is a strong, heroic image and has been used many times, as for example in *Mad Max* (1979) or *Dirty Harry* (1971).

Even though he had only made $100 on his first film, and just broken even on his second, Kubrick had proved to himself that he could make films. He then made an important life decision by quitting his job at *Look* to work full-time as a film-maker. He visited film professionals in New York and asked them detailed and comprehensive questions about the technical aspects of film-making. With no job to support Toba and himself, some weeks the only income Kubrick had was from the chess matches he played in Washington Square – he could make around $3.00 a day. Many people have made the observation that chess requires logic, order and strategy, which are the tools a film-maker needs to bring to a project. In chess each situation must be assessed coolly before any move is made – this is reportedly an attitude that Kubrick brought to his film work.

The confident, and some would say cocksure, Stanley Kubrick felt he had served his apprenticeship and was ready to make his own feature-length film. He had a long and ponderous script written by high school friend Howard O. Sackler, whom Kubrick described as a "poet". (Sackler later won a Pulitzer Prize

"*Among a great many other things that chess teaches you is to control the initial excitement you feel when you see something that looks good. It trains you to think before grabbing, and to think just as objectively when you're in trouble. When you're making a film… a few seconds' thought can often prevent a serious mistake being made about something that looks good at first glance.*"

Stanley Kubrick [1]

ABOVE
On the set of 'Dr Strangelove' (1964)
'The Master', as Kubrick was known in Washington Square Park, keeps an eye on his opponent, George C. Scott.

OPPOSITE
Stanley Kubrick
The intensity of Kubrick's stare often withered all opposition. His single-mindedness, combined with his intellect, helped him to progress within the film business.

On the set of 'Fear and Desire' (1953)
Kubrick prepares to film a scene. Note the branch held in front of the camera.

for his play *The Great White Hope*.) Showing the shorts to his friends and family, Kubrick managed to acquire $1,000 for *The Trap*, as it was first called. His uncle Martin Perveler, who owned a number of businesses in the Los Angeles area, invested a further $9,000 in exchange for an Executive Producer credit. With money in the bank Kubrick assembled his actors and a small crew then flew to the San Gabriel Mountains outside Los Angeles for a five-week shoot. The film is an allegorical tale of four soldiers who survive a plane crash only to find themselves behind enemy lines. On their way back home through the woods, a woman stumbles across them and is killed by a demented young soldier who lusts after her. After they spot an enemy General and his troops, they assassinate the General but find that he and the other soldiers look just like them. They drift to safety on a raft, each of the soldiers either dead or broken by the experience.

It was important to Kubrick that he got the shots he wanted, regardless of what he had to do to get it. For example, he wanted a fog, so he arranged for a crop sprayer to drop insecticide over the location – it almost killed everyone. To speed up the location work and reduce costs he decided to film without sound, but his idea backfired. Kubrick found that adding sound, effects and music increased the total cost to over $50,000 and he needed somebody to bail him out. Successful producer Richard de Rochemont was impressed by the young

Still from 'Fear and Desire' (1953)
Sidney (Paul Mazursky) goes wild and shoots
the girl in a violent attack that predates the
assault on the writer's wife in 'A Clockwork
Orange' (1971).

Kubrick and came to the financial aid of *The Trap*. (It was also called *The Shape of Fear* before finally becoming *Fear and Desire*.) Rochemont was producing a five-part television series about Abraham Lincoln written by James Agee, and he knew director Norman Foster needed some help with location work. As a result, Kubrick and a small team spent some time in Hodgenville, Kentucky casting children, dressing sets and shooting silent film. This assignment helped Kubrick survive a lean time and gave him more experience working with a crew. Returning to New York, he then had to concentrate on getting *Fear and Desire* shown on a public screen.

Although Kubrick later called it a "a bumbling amateur film exercise", *Fear and Desire* was a remarkable achievement for an independent film-maker before such a beast existed. There were only fourteen people on the shoot: five cast, five crew and four Mexicans who transported the equipment, but it was Kubrick who held everything together. While Toba acted as secretary and did the accounts, Kubrick produced, directed, photographed and edited. Although reviewers had mixed feelings about Kubrick's direction, all of them were impressed by the images he composed. The *New York Times* reviewer wrote: 'Mr Kubrick's professionalism as a photographer should be obvious to an amateur. He has artistically caught glimpses of the grotesque attitudes of death,

"Fear and Desire *was a lousy feature, very self-conscious, easily discernible as an intellectual effort, but very roughly, and poorly, and ineffectively made."*

Stanley Kubrick [4]

27

the wolfishness of hungry men as well as their bestiality, and in one scene, the wracking effect of lust on a pitifully juvenile soldier and the pinioned girl he is guarding.'[9] Mark Van Doren, the noted Columbia professor, wrote to Kubrick: 'The incident of the girl bound to a tree will make movie history once it is seen; it is at once beautiful, terrifying and weird; nothing like it has ever been done in a film before, and it alone guarantees that the future of Stanley Kubrick is worth watching for those who want to discover high talent at the moment it appears.'

Stanley Kubrick may have been talented but he had difficulty finding anybody who was willing to pay to see his talent in action. Consequently, he was grateful for anything he was offered. This probably explains why he worked on *The Seafarers*. This was a thirty-minute promotional film for the Seafarers International Union, which was filmed in full colour in June 1953 – it was Kubrick's first film in colour. Supervised by the *Seafarers Log* (the union magazine), Kubrick's role as cinematographer and director was to follow the script and make it look interesting. The film is devoid of cinematic tricks but it does have a scene at the end when a speaker gives an impassioned talk from the podium as the labourers look on. This montage of speaker and audience echoes similar chest-thumping scenes in *Strike* (1924) and *October* (1927), which were directed by Sergei Eisenstein.

Work was difficult to find and Kubrick seemed to drift from one project and idea to another. In 1954, whilst still married to Toba Metz, Kubrick began an affair with Ruth Sobotka, a dancer with the New York City Ballet. He visited her at rehearsals, saw her performances and partied with the troupe. Eventually "cupcake", as Ruth affectionately called him, moved in with her at 222 East Tenth Street, where he planned his next film.

Encouraged by the reviews for *Fear and Desire*, Kubrick sketched out a few scenes for a new movie about a boxer in peril using material and ideas from his previous work with Walter Cartier. *Fear and Desire* had failed to recoup its budget, so Kubrick thought it prudent to ask for further investments from elsewhere. When there was a hint of some cash, Kubrick spent a week or two writing a film noir script with Howard O. Sackler variously titled *Kiss Me, Kill Me* and *The Nymph and the Maniac*. *Killer's Kiss*, as it was eventually called, was the story of two losers, a boxer and a taxi-dancer (she is hired to dance with customers in the same way as the boxer is hired to 'dance' with men), who try to escape their low-rent no-hope lives to be with each other. Eventually Bronx pharmacist Morris Bousel put up $40,000 and Kubrick began his new film. Without permission to film on the streets of New York with his non-union crew, Kubrick resorted to guerrilla tactics and subterfuge. This was nothing new for him because when on assignment for *Look* he had often disguised his camera and still got good images in lousy light. Kubrick shot sequences on Times Square with the actors performing and passers-by not realising they were being filmed. When filming on Wall Street in the early hours of the morning, the crew suddenly found themselves surrounded by policemen. Kubrick calmly handed out $20 to each of the policemen and carried on filming.

Kubrick was developing his own method of film-making, which grew out of his working practices as a photographer. He liked to walk into an environment and roam around it to find the angles and images he wanted. To recreate this environment, Kubrick spent his time lighting the sets. The importance of

ABOVE
Still from 'Fear and Desire' (1953)
Steve Coit and Kenneth Harp play their characters' doppelgängers. Twins and reflections in mirrors reoccur throughout Kubrick's films.

OPPOSITE
On the set of 'Killer's Kiss' (1955)
A portrait of the young film-maker. Note the shooting script in Kubrick's shirt pocket.

Still from 'Killer's Kiss' (1955)
The innocent and naïve relationship between Davy Gordon (Jamie Smith) and Gloria Price (Irene Kane) is symbolised by the doll they clutch.

the images to Kubrick can be seen in his response to the technical problems he encountered on *Killer's Kiss*. Concerned that he would be hit with vast post-production bills, as with *Fear and Desire*, Kubrick decided to record the sound on location. However, the microphones were on booms, so they cast shadows and restricted camera movement. Kubrick decided that rather than compromise the images he would film without sound. It was a costly decision. After the 12–14 week shoot, Kubrick spent seven months and an additional $35,000 adding the sound.

The film has a very simple plot, like all of Kubrick's films. Boxer Davy Gordon lives alone in a flat, as does the beautiful girl he can see living across the courtyard from him. Their lives are blighted – as Davy is knocked out in the ring that night, Gloria is forcibly kissed by her slimy boss Vincent Rapallo, who is jealous of all the men who pay to dance with her at the dance hall. Later, after Gloria is sexually harassed by Vincent in her apartment, Davy stays the night to protect her. The couple find comfort in each other and decide to escape their dark lives using the money from Davy's fight. When Davy's manager waits outside the dance hall to give Davy the money, he is mistaken for Davy and killed by Vincent's henchmen. Gloria is kidnapped by Vincent, so Davy gets a gun and races after the kidnappers to rescue her. After

Still from 'Killer's Kiss' (1955)
Gloria grooms herself whilst reflecting on her
father and sister (Ruth Sobotka), seen in the
photos on her bureau.

an exciting chase across the rooftops of derelict buildings, Vincent and Davy
end up fighting in a mannequin warehouse, where Davy kills Vincent with
a mannequin leg. Free of their past, the young lovers kiss in a train station,
destined for a brighter future.

The use of mannequins is both unusual and appropriate to the theme of
the film, which is about how the central characters become other people's
puppets and are made to act against their will. For example, Davy is paid to
be violent when it is obvious that he is a sensitive man. Also, Gloria is forced
to dance with men for money (and there are sexual overtones to this business
as well – she is a sex toy) and despises it. At one point, when Gloria sleeps
there is a cut to a doll in the same position. This obvious piece of symbolism
hints at the influence of Sergei Eisenstein, who often showed visual metaphors
for his characters. Again the same symbolism is used in the mannequin warehouse, when we see Davy's head as one of three faces in a row – the other
two being mannequins. Seen in this context, the end sequence can be read as
the 'puppets' fighting back. I'm sure that the symbolism and black humour of
the manager of a dance hall being killed by a leg was not lost on the writers.

Although, like *Fear and Desire*, the film suffered from some mediocre
acting, there was no denying its visual flair. The boxing sequences recreated

Still from 'Killer's Kiss' (1955)
Davy takes a beating in this realistic bout, inspired by Kubrick's previous work with boxer Walter Cartier in the photo essay 'Prizefighter' (1949) and the documentary 'Day of the Fight' (1951).

atmospheric shots and exciting angles from *Day of the Fight*, and influenced Martin Scorsese's *Raging Bull* (1980). As well as finding new angles, Kubrick was not shy about using ideas from other directors. The idea of a painting laughing at a character was used in Alfred Hitchcock's *Blackmail* (1929). Another Hitchcock reference occurs when Vincent is killed – Vincent screams, we see a mannequin's mouth and then hear a train whistle. This is very similar to the discovery of the dead woman at the beginning of *The 39 Steps* (1936). However, there are many camera movements, techniques and subjects that would soon be identified as Kubrickian – characters moving through corridors, symmetrical framing, film noir lighting and angles, hand-held camerawork, hand-to-hand fighting, dysfunctional families and staring eyes.

Killer's Kiss was an incredible achievement for an independent film-maker (Kubrick sold it to United Artists for $75,000, barely making back the money spent on it) but it showed a basic flaw in Kubrick's film-making skills – it had a weak story with weak characters. Kubrick did not make the same mistake again and every subsequent film he made had a strong literary source.

However, there would be some important changes in Kubrick's life before he could make better films.

ABOVE
Still from 'Killer's Kiss' (1955)
Davy in a mannequin warehouse, a surreal
place that is a metaphor for the real world where
Davy and Gloria sell their bodies.

PAGES 34/35
Still from 'Killer's Kiss' (1955)
The bizarre fight sequence between Vincent
(Frank Silvera) and Davy.

*"If a film has any substance or subtlety, whatever
you say is never complete, it's usually wrong, and
it's necessarily simplistic: truth is too multifaceted
to be contained in a five-line summary. If the
work is good, what you say about it is usually
irrelevant."*

Stanley Kubrick [31]

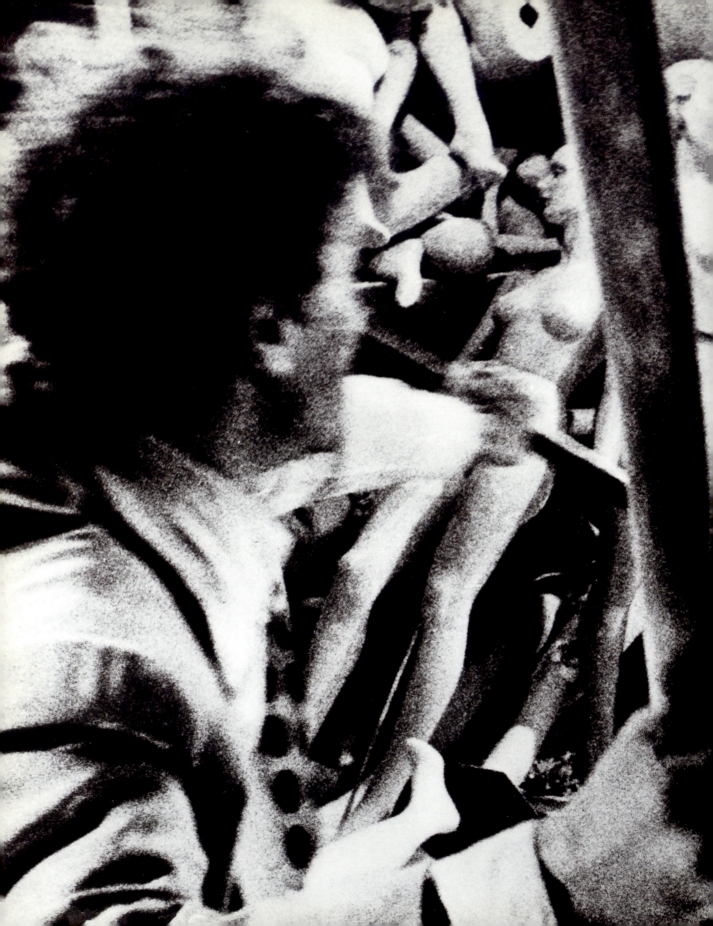

How Stanley Kubrick paid his dues to Hollywood

Although *Killer's Kiss* was a step up from *Fear and Desire*, people were still not knocking on Kubrick's door offering him work and a blank cheque. The few dollars he won playing chess in Washington Square came in useful while he explored different avenues. It was at this point that he met James B. Harris. Harris and Alex Singer had become friends in the Signal Corps during the Korean War and upon their return Harris met Kubrick. Harris said that Kubrick "was the most intelligent, most creative person I had ever come in contact with." It soon became clear that they could help each other. Harris had co-owned and subsequently sold a successful film distribution company but now he wanted to become a producer and needed a talent to produce. Kubrick had made two films but needed a producer to handle financing whilst he concentrated on making movies. This mutual need led to the formation of the Harris-Kubrick Pictures Corporation in 1955.

The new team needed a property to film. Harris bought and read *Clean Break* by Lionel White, a novel about a racetrack robbery. He liked it because it was told from different points of view at different times, like Akira Kurosawa's film *Rashomon* (1950). Dipping into his savings, Harris bought the rights for $10,000 just ahead of United Artists, who were interested in the property for Frank Sinatra as a follow-on to his successful thriller *Suddenly* (1954). Kubrick decided which scenes were to be used and, upon Kubrick's suggestion, they employed noir novelist Jim Thompson to write the script. Thompson, author of the chilling *The Killer Inside Me* (1952), added important elements to the story like the sadomasochistic relationship between George and his man-eating wife Sherry.

With the script complete, Kubrick was wary that Harris, who had put a lot of his own money into the script and wanted to make sure he got it back, might bow to pressure from a studio if they wanted to axe Kubrick and bring in an experienced director. Harris told Kubrick "my philosophy was that when you select your partner you live or die with your partner. And that's the way it was."[10]

United Artists said that if Harris-Kubrick got a big actor for *The Killing*, as it was renamed, they would put up some money. After copies were mailed to

On the set of 'Spartacus' (1960)
Stanley Kubrick quietly explains what he wants from Kirk Douglas.

"A director is a kind of idea and taste machine."
Stanley Kubrick[5]

Still from 'The Killing' (1956)
The nervous little man George Peatty (Elisha Cook, Jr.) watches as mastermind Johnny (Sterling Hayden) outlines the robbery to the gang. Marvin Unger (Jay C. Flippen, right) is the money man.

"...a criminal film...is almost like a bullfight: it has a ritual and a pattern which lays down that the criminal is not going to make it."

Stanley Kubrick [24]

every leading actor in Hollywood, Sterling Hayden (the lead in *The Asphalt Jungle* and Kubrick's first choice for the role) said he'd do it for $40,000. He wasn't big enough for United Artists, so they only put up $200,000. Harris added $80,000 of his own money and loaned $50,000 from his father to complete the financing. Kubrick, his wife Ruth (they married on 15 January 1955 after Kubrick divorced Toba in 1954), Harris and Singer moved from New York to film in L. A. Kubrick was not paid and lived off loans from Harris whilst Ruth, who had designed ballets and stage productions, designed the sets and drew storyboards for the film. Kubrick cast the film from character actors he had remembered from the hundreds of films noirs he had seen: slimy Timothy Carey; tough Ted de Corsica; wimpy Elisha Cook Jr.; and vampish Marie Windsor. The dignified wrestler was played by Kubrick's old chess buddy Kola Kwariani.

Although he had brought some of his own people with him and was quite happy to do everything himself, Kubrick now had to contend with the Hollywood machine. The union said that Kubrick could not be the cinematographer, so veteran Lucien Ballard was brought in. Hollywood cinematographers were the masters of their own tight-knit crews and usually talked to the director then made all the technical decisions. This was not Kubrick's

way. On one occasion Kubrick set up a long tracking shot – he placed the camera close to the actors and used a 25mm wide angle lens which slightly distorted the image. Ballard then moved the camera away from the actors and set it up with a 50mm lens. Kubrick, who was only 27, asserted his authority and, without resorting to histrionics, quietly told Ballard to move the camera back or he was off the film.

The Killing has many of the key components of the heist movie but Kubrick plays with our expectations. The gang are not hardened criminals but people who represent all walks of life: policeman Randy; accountant George; labourer Mike; intellectual/artist Maurice; fighter Nikki; waster Marvin; and gangster/leader Johnny. Each of them has their own motivation for wanting the money: Randy has gambling debts; George needs to look after his high-maintenance wife; Mike's wife is sick and needs treatment; Johnny has just come out of jail and needs one last score for his retirement; Marvin is in love with Johnny which is why he puts up the money. When the gang assemble to go over the plan they end up fighting among themselves, but at the racetrack robbery the gang – this mini-society – work together. Finally there is the getaway that goes horribly wrong with dead bodies littering the floor. This 'moral' ending is foreshadowed when Maurice (the artist) tells Johnny (the gangster) at the

ABOVE
Still from 'The Killing' (1956)
George and his high-maintenance wife Sherry (Marie Windsor) have a sadomasochistic relationship. When she hears that George is part of a robbery, she and her boyfriend plan to steal the money from the robbers.

PAGES 40/41
Still from 'The Killing' (1956)
Nikki (Timothy Carey) is the arrogant hitman who enjoys his work. In this case he has to shoot a horse during an important race to distract the police away from the robbery.

Still from 'The Killing' (1956)
The wrestler Maurice Oboukhoff (played by Kubrick's chess friend Kola Kwariani) creates a diversion.

chess club: "I often thought that the gangster and the artist are the same in the eyes of the masses. They are admired and hero-worshipped, but there is always present an underlying wish to see them destroyed at the peak of their glory."

Like other heist movies, this is a meticulous, step-by-step, chess-like explanation of how everything that man does is doomed to failure because of his self-destructive impulses. Johnny spends the whole of the movie trying to achieve something, but it is all for nothing. This is succinctly summed up by his last words in the film, "What's the difference?" Life is a game of chance that we cannot control. We try to stack the odds in our favour but it cannot be done. The film is set against the background of gambling to emphasise this – the gang steal money that people have bet and lost. At the beginning we see Marvin discard his losing tickets on the floor of the betting office, which is littered with thousands of losing tickets. Later we see the dead bodies of the main characters, littering the floor like those losing tickets. And at the end, the lost money covers the airport runway. The film seems to be saying, 'we all end up as food for the worms so why bother trying to do anything at all?'

The Killing failed to get a proper release and, at the last minute, was put in playing second feature to *Bandido!* (1956). It didn't make any money but it did get some favourable reviews. *Time* said that 'the camera watches the whole shoddy show with the keen eye of a terrier stalking a pack of rats,' and even compared *The Killing* to the work of Orson Welles. Clearly, Harris and Kubrick thought, they had registered their presence in Hollywood. This was not the case according to Max Youngstein at United Artists. When the two young hotshots cornered Youngstein and asked him where they stood in relation to other new talent, Youngstein replied, "Not far from the bottom."

Harris and Kubrick had signed to The Jaffe Agency, who consequently screened *The Killing* at different studios. Dore Schary at MGM thought enough of the movie to give Harris and Kubrick a deal – the team would get $75,000 to write, direct and produce a film. Schary asked if they had anything in mind. They had the film rights to *Paths of Glory*.

ABOVE
Still from 'The Killing' (1956)
The mask Johnny (Sterling Hayden) wears during the hold-up is similar to the masks used by Alex and his droogs in 'A Clockwork Orange' (1971).

LEFT
Still from 'The Killing' (1956)
Johnny makes his getaway during the robbery.

PAGES 44/45
Still from 'The Killing' (1956)
George lies dead, free at last. He had been as trapped in life as a bird in a cage.

Still from 'Paths of Glory' (1957)
Colonel Dax (Kirk Douglas) marches determinedly through the trenches, thinking that he has power. The reverse tracking shot is one Kubrick used often.

"I've always liked moving the camera. When you have the means to do it and the set to do it in, it not only adds visual interest but it also permits the actors to work in longer, possibly complete, takes. This makes it easier for them to maintain their concentration and emotional level in the scene."

Stanley Kubrick [1]

Many years earlier, Kubrick had read Humphrey Cobb's 1935 novel *Paths of Glory* while waiting in his father's office. Cobb, a veteran of World War One, based the book on the true story of five French soldiers who had been shot for mutiny in 1915 and were then cleared of the charges in 1934 – one of the widows got one franc compensation. Schary was familiar with the property and said that MGM would not finance it because they had just done an anti-war movie, *The Red Badge of Courage* (1951). So Harris, Kubrick, Alex Singer and Gavin Lambert spent weeks sifting through the properties owned by MGM and found *The Burning Secret* by Stefan Zweig – one of Kubrick's favourite directors, Max Ophüls, had made *Letter from an Unknown Woman* (1948) from a Zweig story. During the day Kubrick worked on a script for *The Burning Secret* with novelist Calder Willingham, and the evenings were spent illegally working on a first draft of *Paths of Glory* with Jim Thompson. When Schary left MGM, Harris and Kubrick were fired because they had been working on *Paths of Glory*, a non-MGM project. Harris was happy to concentrate full-time on *Paths of Glory*.

   The original script by Thompson and Kubrick had Colonel Dax blackmail a superior and save the lives of the three soldiers. Kubrick wanted a happy ending so that the film would be commercial, but the later script rewrites by Calder Willingham restored the pessimism of the original novel and made Colonel

Still from 'Paths of Glory' (1957)
Colonel Dax leads his men forward. The French
soldiers' mission to capture the German 'Ant Hill'
is impossible and is undertaken for purely
political reasons.

Dax more powerful with each version. Kirk Douglas wanted to play Colonel
Dax, and Harris-Kubrick were so desperate to get the film made that they signed
a five-picture deal with Douglas' Bryna Productions. Douglas told United Artists
that he would not do their guaranteed money-earner *The Vikings* (1958) unless
they took *Paths of Glory* and paid $850,000 to make it. It was obvious who had
the power: Douglas got $350,000; Harris and Kubrick worked for $20,000 plus
a percentage of the profits. The production moved to Munich, Germany, in
January 1957 where, after shooting a scene full of swirling camera movements,
Kubrick told actor Richard Anderson that Max Ophüls had died that day and
that the shots were in his honour. Clearly the smooth camera movements
Kubrick uses throughout the film are an emulation of Ophüls' style but they
also serve a purpose. The camera is our fluid eye, following and anticipating the
movements of the characters.

Paths of Glory* opens at a luxurious château, where General Paul Mireau and
his superior, General George Broulard, circle each other as a visual metaphor
for their verbal dual. George explains that the *Ant Hill* – fortified German
trenches overlooking the French trenches – has to be taken and hints that a pro-
motion could be in the offing for Paul. The swirling movements in the château
are replaced by straight, direct movements of the camera in the trenches, and

then in the battlefield, where Colonel Dax leads his men to certain death and defeat. General Mireau is outraged that 'B' company does not attack and orders his own artillery to bomb it – Captain Rousseau refuses to do so without written orders. Kubrick shows the people in command, Broulard and Dax, walking through the trenches from left to right, which is psychologically strong, but the soldiers attack on the *Ant Hill* moving from right to left, which is psychologically weak and feels as though they are climbing uphill.

After the retreat, the generals want to set an example, so three men are picked for execution by the company commanders. Colonel Dax, who was a criminal lawyer in civilian life, defends the men but it is a foregone conclusion that the soldiers will die. The indictment is not read out because it would waste time. Dax protests at the absurdity of the court martial, that there are no witnesses for the prosecution and there is no stenographer making a record of the trial. After the predetermined verdict is given, the prisoners are ceremonially led to poles and shot.

We can see that the château is the generals' battleground. The château's marble floor is chequered like a chessboard, making the soldiers appear to be pawns in the generals' power game. The court martial and execution at the château are very formal and symmetrical, with the soldiers arranged in ranks. This gives the impression of order and control, in direct contrast to the chaos of trench warfare, yet both are forms of senseless murder. This is a society that is inexorably destroying itself.

Kubrick shows us the monstrous indifference of the generals both verbally and visually. After they are sentenced, the prisoners eat nothing for their last meal because the food is drugged, whilst the officers eat from a large table and dance a waltz in the room where the court martial was held. And after the execution, as the two generals eat General Mireau comments, "The men died wonderfully. There is always a chance that one will do something that will leave a bad taste in your mouth."

Dax tells General Broulard that Mireau had ordered his own men to be bombed and Mireau is subsequently relieved of his command. Dax is offered Mireau's command, since Broulard assumes it was Dax's motive for passing on the information. When he realises that Dax really did want to save the men, Broulard pities Dax for his idealism and sentimentality. It is at this point that Dax is most disillusioned with the world.

The film could very well have ended there, leaving a bad taste in the mouth, but Kubrick and Willingham, who had been furiously rewriting dialogue during filming, came up with a more upbeat ending. They wrote a scene where Dax watches the men laugh and jeer at a German girl put on the stage at a drinking hall. Then she sings a German folk song and the beauty of it touches them all. Earlier, the prosecutor Saint-Auban said he thought of the soldiers as lower animals but Dax disagreed, saying that they were humans. Hearing the soldiers sing along with the girl, Dax realises that he was right and that he is fighting for humanity.

The German girl was played by Susanne Christian, a young actress whom Kubrick had begun dating. Kubrick's marriage to Ruth had effectively ended when he remained in Los Angeles and she had to return to New York to resume rehearsals with the New York City Ballet – they divorced in 1957. Susanne,

ABOVE
Still from 'Paths of Glory' (1957)
The cordial banter of Generals Mireau (George Macready) and Broulard (Adolphe Menjou) hides a wealth of political intrigue.

OPPOSITE
Still from 'Paths of Glory' (1957)
Colonel Dax experiences the Hell of trench warfare.

ABOVE
On the set of 'Paths of Glory' (1957)
Susanne Christian, Stanley Kubrick and Kirk Douglas enjoy a hot drink in the Munich cold. Susanne Christian became Kubrick's lifelong partner.

OPPOSITE TOP
Still from 'Paths of Glory' (1957)
General Mireau surveys his troops in the trenches, accompanied by Major Saint-Auban (Richard Anderson).

OPPOSITE BOTTOM
Still from 'Paths of Glory' (1957)
The three scapegoats, Férol (Timothy Carey), Corporal Paris (Ralph Meeker) and Arnaud (Joseph Turkel), sit in the courtroom waiting to be found guilty.

whose real name is Christiane Harlan, became Kubrick's third wife and lifetime partner in 1958.

When *Paths of Glory* was released it caused controversy around the world. It was banned in France until 1974. It was withdrawn from the Berlin Film Festival. It was censored by the Swiss Army until 1970. The US military banned it from its European bases.

The critics were more enthusiastic. Bosley Crowther of the *New York Times* wrote that 'The close, hard eye of Mr Kubrick's sullen camera bores directly into the minds of scheming men and into the hearts of patient, frightened soldiers who have to accept orders to die.' In *Sight and Sound*, Gavin Lambert suggested that 'its epigraph might be von Clausewitz's remark: war is merely an extension of the policies of peace' and that 'by showing the gulf between leaders and led fatally widened by the fact of war, [it] shows war... as an extended struggle for power, internal and external. It is the practical as opposed to the sentimental argument.'

Although *Paths of Glory* has since been recognised as Kubrick's first masterpiece, not many people paid money to see it, so Harris and Kubrick languished for a couple of years trying to get their next project made. They developed a sitcom starring Ernie Kovacs and a film of the book *I Stole $16,000,000* by real-life criminal Herbert Emerson Wilson, but nothing came of these projects. Marlon Brando rang up and asked Kubrick to direct *The Authentic Death of Hendry Jones*, from a western novel by Charles Neider based on the story of lawman Pat Garrett and outlaw Billy the Kid. There were so many changes and so many opinions (Brando stopped arguments by banging a gong) that it became very messy. In the end, Kubrick was fired and Brando took over the directorial chores of *One-Eyed Jacks* (1961) as it was renamed.

During the summer of 1958 when Kubrick suffered one interminable meeting after another on *One-Eyed Jacks*, Kubrick and Harris had fallen in love with the best-selling novel *Lolita* by Vladimir Nabokov. When they received a copy in the office, Kubrick was so anxious to read it that Harris tore out the pages he had read and handed them to Kubrick. When they finished, they knew they had to make it into a movie. They acquired the screen rights at a cost of $150,000 by optioning their share of *The Killing* and then approached the censor about how they could make the story of a man in love with a young girl acceptable to audiences. They couldn't find a solution. Before beginning work on the script, Kubrick got a phone call from Kirk Douglas on Friday 13 February 1959 saying that he needed him to direct a film starting Monday – he had a weekend to get up to speed with *Spartacus*.

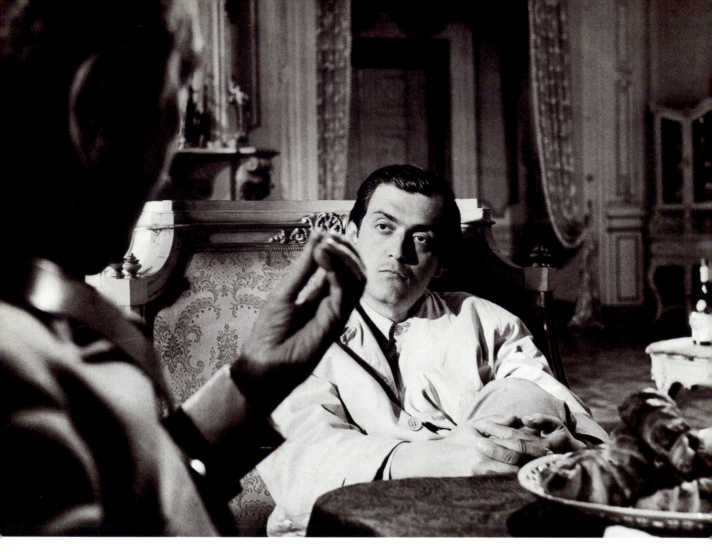

ABOVE
On the set of 'Paths of Glory' (1957)
The experienced actor Adolphe Menjou (left) was angry that Kubrick repeatedly asked him to do a scene and complained for some time. When he had finished, Kubrick calmly asked him to do another take.

RIGHT
On the set of 'Paths of Glory' (1957)
Susanne Christian with some of the actors. Eight hundred German policemen were employed to play French soldiers.

ABOVE
On the set of 'Paths of Glory' (1957)
Stanley Kubrick discusses the next courtroom shot with producer James B. Harris and Kirk Douglas.

LEFT
On the set of 'Paths of Glory' (1957)
Kirk Douglas and Stanley Kubrick run through a scene in the bunker.

"Stanley is unusually perceptive, and delicately attuned to people. He has an adroit intellect, and is a creative thinker – not a repeater, not a fact-gatherer. He digests what he learns and brings to a new project an original point of view and a reserved passion."

Marlon Brando

On the set of 'Paths of Glory' (1957)
Kirk Douglas, Adolphe Menjou, George
Macready and Richard Anderson patiently
wait for the execution to be filmed.

On the set of 'Paths of Glory' (1957)
Kirk Douglas.

ABOVE
Still from 'Paths of Glory' (1957)
The three soldiers are shot. The rows of
men and the symmetrical composition of
Kubrick's framing suggest that the world
of the château is ordered, but it is just as
chaotic and murderous as the trenches.

RIGHT
Still from 'Paths of Glory' (1957)
General Broulard dances and has all the
accoutrements of civilisation around him,
but he is barbaric in thought and deed.

ABOVE
Still from 'Paths of Glory' (1957)
The execution from the point of view of the firing squad. The composition remains symmetrical and formal in direct contract to the chaos of the attack on the German 'Ant Hill'.

LEFT
Still from 'Paths of Glory' (1957)
The final scene features a German girl whose singing turns the jeers of the French soldiers into tears. Watching this renews Colonel Dax's faith in human nature.

When Kirk Douglas acquired the rights to Howard Fast's novel *Spartacus*, he hired blacklisted writer Dalton Trumbo to do the screenplay. Trumbo had been on the blacklist for ten years after the House Un-American Activities Committee put him in jail for a year for failing to name names in the infamous Communist witch-hunt. Incredibly, Trumbo had won an Oscar for *The Brave One* in 1956, writing under the pseudonym Robert Rich. Douglas' Bryna Productions had several blacklisted writers working for it at cheap rates, as did many other production companies. The reliable and experienced Anthony Mann was hired to direct *Spartacus* at Universal Studios' insistence because the movie had an enormous budget of $6 million. Mann, who was adept at bringing out the most sensitive emotions of complex characters, was happy to take suggestions from Peter Ustinov and the other English actors, Laurence Olivier and Charles Laughton, and consequently tried to elicit a more subtle performance from Douglas. Douglas, whose acting style was more physical and instinctive, feared he was losing control of the production and fired Mann on Friday 13 February. He phoned Kubrick who, after a weekend of negotiations, came on board for $150,000 and brokered a deal with Bryna Productions that allowed Harris-Kubrick to retain *Lolita*.

The story begins with Spartacus, a Thracian born into slavery and sold to the mines of Libya at the age of 13, being bought by Lentulus Batiatus and trained to be a gladiator. Spartacus falls in love with Varinia and makes friends with the Ethiopian Draba. When Spartacus and Draba are forced to fight to the death for the sport of Crassus and his friends from Rome, Draba defeats Spartacus but refuses to kill him, then attacks the Romans and is killed. The next day, when Spartacus learns that Varinia has been sold to Crassus, he leads the gladiators in an escape to the hills. The gladiators take up residence on Mount Vesuvius, where they are joined by thousands of slaves including Varinia (who becomes pregnant) and Antoninus, an educated slave of Crassus to whom Crassus revealed his bisexuality.

The gladiators train the other former slaves and the slave army defeats the Roman cohorts. With the people of Rome afraid for their lives, Crassus and Gracchus fight for the leadership of the city. The slaves pay pirates to take them away from Italy but Crassus bribes the pirates not to – Crassus wants to defeat the slave army so that he can become dictator of Rome. The slaves are slaughtered by Crassus' army in a long and bloody battle, then Crassus offers to spare all 6,000 prisoners from crucifixion if they reveal which of them is Spartacus. As Spartacus rises to save their lives, all the slaves rise to identify themselves as Spartacus – they are all crucified. Spartacus is the last to be crucified, at the gates of Rome. As Batiatus smuggles Varinia and her child out of Rome with Gracchus' help, Varinia shows Spartacus his son – his son is free.

In outline, *Spartacus* advocates the democratic rights of individuals. Spartacus' uprising is a physical symbol that everybody has the right to decide their own future. The debates and manoeuvres of Crassus and Gracchus in the Senate show the political dimension of this position. Crassus believes that the elite know what is best for everybody and that they should rule as a benevolent dictatorship. Gracchus believes in democracy but that the slaves simply have no idea how to rule society once their changes have been completed. The film ends with both Spartacus and Gracchus dead, and the dictator Crassus controlling the world.

Publicity still for 'Spartacus' (1960)
Spartacus' spirit has been trained and honed to make him a killing machine.

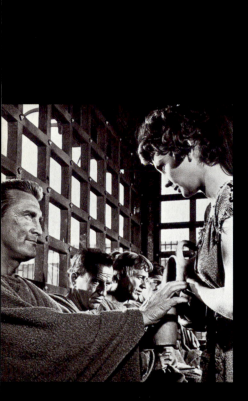

Given that Fast and Trumbo were its writers this could be read as an allegory
for the oppression of Senator McCarthy and the House Un-American Activities
Committee.

Laurence Olivier gives a sly, sensuous performance as Crassus, who is the
most interesting character in the movie, mainly because he is a villain whose
motives are understandable. (Peter Ustinov won the Best Supporting Actor
Oscar for his role as Lentulus Batiatus.) Crassus is rich and powerful, and he
believes it is his birthright to lead. His fanatical patriotism and love for Rome
are real and are given sexual connotations – he talks of not entering her with
his army because that would violate her laws.

The sexual dimension to his character is reinforced by sauna and bathing
scenes. In the sauna scene Crassus lures Julius Caesar away from Gracchus,
and in a bathing scene Crassus reveals his desire for Antoninus. When Crassus
professes his love for both Varinia and Antoninus, but that love is not returned,
his desire to possess Rome grows even more desperate. The fact that Varinia
and Antoninus run away to be with Spartacus makes it appear that Crassus
is not only defending his beloved Rome but revenging himself on previous
loves who had spurned him. This is certainly the implication when he forces
Spartacus and Antoninus to fight to the death.

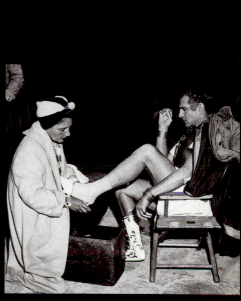

As on *The Killing*, Kubrick found it difficult working with the Hollywood veterans, who had a regimented way of working. At least on *Paths of Glory* he had been able to take the production to Germany and found a freedom to direct. There is a famous incident where Kubrick walked onto a set that had been lit by cinematographer Russell Metty. Kubrick said there was not enough light, at which Metty got angry and kicked a light onto the set. "Now there is too much," Kubrick said calmly.

Kubrick also found working with Kirk Douglas difficult and their working relationship suffered. Although Douglas had employed Kubrick because he thought that perhaps he would be grateful and pliable to a certain degree, Kubrick in fact was probably more determined than Anthony Mann.

Filming was beset with problems. Jean Simmons needed emergency surgery, Douglas was often late on set and had a ten-day virus, Ustinov, Olivier and Laughton all had pressing commitments around the world, and Tony Curtis was in plaster for weeks after spraining an Achilles tendon. In addition Trumbo was doing rewrites every day. Consequently, Kubrick adopted a new working method – he improvised on set with the actors and carved performances rather than totally relying on the script. If there was no dialogue for a scene then Kubrick played mood music, just like in the silent days, to convey the emotion of a scene. This worked to great effect, especially in the scene where Spartacus and Draba wait to go into the arena to fight. He played a Prokofiev concerto on the close-up on Woody Strode.

Kubrick used some of his camera movements and ideas from *Paths of Glory*. For example, the reverse tracking when Batiatus walks in the Libyan mines and Spartacus reviews the former slaves the night before the big attack, are echoes of the walks Colonel Dax and General Broulard make through the trenches in *Paths of Glory*. The Senate floor is chequered in black and white, like the marble floor of the château. Also, for the big battle scene in *Spartacus*, Kubrick cuts to the exact drum beats, which heightens the tension, just as in the execution scene at the end of *Paths of Glory*. The gladiator is a performer and his fight to the death is a type of play, with the circular arena as his theatre. Kubrick uses the circular arena as a symbol throughout the movie. When the gladiators escape, they force some Romans to fight in the gladiatorial arena but Spartacus is repulsed by this and stops them, asking: "Are we animals?" This echoes Saint-Auban's line about soldiers being lower animals in *Paths of Glory*. Later, when Glabrus and his cohorts are overthrown, the Roman commander stands inside a circle of rebels. At the end, Spartacus fights Antoninus to the death in a circle of Roman soldiers.

Virtually all the film was shot on the Universal Studios backlot with some locations in Death Valley, by the sea and six weeks in Spain to shoot the climactic battle sequence. Kubrick was upset by the flight to Spain. He had earned his pilot's licence on 15 August 1947 so that he could travel around the United States and Europe to complete his assignments for *Look* magazine. On one such assignment, he had nearly crashed his plane. Shortly after, as Christiane Kubrick told Nick James, "a colleague was killed piloting a plane and for some reason his camera and notebooks, horribly squashed and burnt, were sent to Kubrick. It traumatised him. But it was only when he flew to Spain to film *Spartacus* that the reaction hit him. Terribly ill, in a state of nervous shock, the return flight was his last [but one]."[11]

After 167 days of filming, Kubrick spent months editing the footage together and trimming it after protests from the Legion of Decency and the Production Code Administration. (The scene where Crassus attempts to seduce Antoninus in the bath was edited back into the 1991 restored version along with several other scenes.) It had been an enormous undertaking, and one he should have been proud of, but in later years he would speak badly of the film, because it was not his own and did not represent his themes and concerns as a film-maker.

Even though Kubrick had proved he could make a big, profitable film – it cost $12 million and took $14.6 million on its first run – the whole experience of being part of the Hollywood machine, of being pulled in all directions by conflicting powers ("If I ever needed any convincing of the limits of persuasion a director can have on a film where someone else is the producer and he is merely the highest-paid member of the crew, *Spartacus* provided proof to last a lifetime,"[12]), of having no control over the creativity of the project ("In *Spartacus* I tried with only limited success to make the film as real as possible but I was up against a pretty dumb script which was rarely faithful to what is known about Spartacus,"[13]), was not one he would ever allow to happen again.

"He'll be a fine director some day, if he falls flat on his face just once. It might teach him how to compromise."

Kirk Douglas

LEFT
Still from 'Spartacus' (1960)
The gladiators escape their Roman captors and make their bid for freedom.

PAGES 66/67
On the set of 'Spartacus' (1960)
Slaves from all over Italy joined the revolt of the gladiators. Kubrick marshals thousands of extras on location in Spain to show this mass migration.

Still from 'Spartacus' (1960)
Gracchus (Charles Laughton) debates with
Julius Caesar (John Gavin) in the Senate.
Note the formal design of the floor, which
echoes the chessboard effect of the château
floor in 'Paths of Glory'.

Stanley Kubrick once said to Shelley Duvall, "Nothing great was ever accomplished without suffering."[1] The suffering that he referred to almost certainly had much to do with his experiences on *Spartacus*. However, it should be remembered that *Spartacus* was also a time of great joy for Kubrick. By the end of filming Kubrick had three daughters: Katharina was Christiane's daughter from a previous marriage; Anya Renata was born just after filming began on 6 April 1959; and Vivian Vanessa was born on 5 August 1960, just before the release of the film.

How Stanley Kubrick gained independence through hard work and determination

Many problems have to be solved to make a film and *Lolita* had more than its fair share. For example, as well as acquiring the film rights to the novel of *Lolita*, Harris-Kubrick acquired the rights to Vladimir Nabokov's *Laughter in the Dark*, which had a similar theme, so that a rival production could not use it. More difficult to solve was how to adapt such a literary and controversial work.

The novel was rejected by American publishers after its completion in 1954 because it was the story of Humbert Humbert, a 39-year-old man, who desired Lolita, a 12-year-old girl. The novel was eventually published in Paris the following year by the Olympia Press and was first published in America in 1958.

The film version was even more troublesome because there was the possibility that the film-makers would actually show what is implied in the book. Novels are usually about words and emotions, both of which are notoriously difficult to translate into film because film relies on visuals and plot. It also has to be borne in mind that the novel was arguably the artistic pinnacle of an author who had been writing for 40 years, and it was being directed by a man half his age who had been in film for 10 years and was still finding his artistic way.

The solutions to these problems and others surrounding the production of *Lolita* led to a series of events that would irrevocably change Kubrick's future. In the year that Kubrick spent directing *Spartacus*, *Lolita* sold almost 300,000 copies in America, and it went on to sell more than 14 million copies worldwide. After originally rejecting the idea of writing the screenplay, Nabokov had second thoughts and moved to Hollywood. The two draft screenplays he wrote from March to September 1960 incorporated ideas and scenes he had not included in the novel. The first draft was four hundred pages, of which Harris commented in 1993, "You couldn't make it. You couldn't *lift* it."

Kubrick and Harris then rewrote the screenplay to fit Kubrick's cinematic vision of the story and to satisfy the censor. With a script in hand, all Harris-Kubrick had to do was sign on the dotted line with Warner Brothers for a $1 million deal and to look forward to 50% of the profits. However, Warner

OPPOSITE
On the set of '2001: A Space Odyssey' (1968)
Stanley Kubrick is behind the camera whilst filming the monolith on the Moon excavation set.

PAGES 74/75
Still from 'Lolita' (1962)
Humbert Humbert (James Mason) looks appreciatively at Lolita (Sue Lyon).

"When you make a movie, it takes a few days just to get used to the crew, because it is like getting undressed in front of fifty people. Once you're accustomed to them, the presence of even one other person on the set is discordant and tends to produce self-consciousness in the actors, and certainly in myself."

Stanley Kubrick [24]

*"You'll see a [chess] grand master, the guy has
three minutes on the clock and ten moves left.
And he'll spend two minutes on one move,
because he knows that if he doesn't get that one
right, the game will be lost. And then he makes the
last nine moves in a minute. Well, in film-making,
you always have decisions like that. You are
always pitting time and resources against quality
and ideas."*

Stanley Kubrick [31]

Brothers had put a phrase into every clause giving Warners complete control
over every aspect of the film. After *Spartacus*, Kubrick and Harris were un-
willing to give up their autonomy and refused to sign. Instead, Harris rapidly
got a $1 million deal for the picture with Eliot Hyman's Associated Artists
that included a clause stating that the company could not touch a frame
of the film. They decided to film in England because the Eady plan allowed
producers to write off the costs if 80% of the crew were English. Luckily
James Mason, who was to play Humbert Humbert, had retained his English
passport but Kubrick needed to find more English talent to meet the quota.
Peter Sellers more than met that quota in his role as Clare Quilty (and his
various disguises).

The film begins with Humbert shooting Clare Quilty in cold blood and
the rest of the story explains what drove Humbert to that action. This introduction gave Kubrick a dramatic framework into which he could place
Humbert and Lolita's relationship. Four years earlier, Humbert began teaching
the French Romantics at Beardsley College and needs a place to stay for the
summer. He is not interested in either the flirtatious Charlotte Haze or her
house but after seeing her daughter Lolita he agrees to rent a room. Humbert
then spends his time in the company of Charlotte and Lolita, surreptitiously
taking delight in any form of physical contact with the young girl. Humbert
marries Charlotte, but when Charlotte dies in an accident Humbert has Lolita
all to himself. They argue constantly because Humbert is jealous of her being
in contact with boys her own age. They go on a road trip but Lolita disappears
in the company of an 'uncle'. Three years later Lolita – older, pregnant and
married to a low-income labourer with a hearing aid – begs Humbert for
money and tells him that she had been in love with another man all along:
Clare Quilty. Quilty pops up in the narrative several times under different disguises, playing with the dogged, unimaginative Humbert. Humbert tracks

down Quilty and shoots him, then dies of a heart attack before his case goes to trial.

The death of Clare Quilty is a manic performance by Peter Sellers, who Kubrick encouraged to improvise on set. ("I'm Spartacus. Have you come to free the slaves or something?" Quilty exclaims, in an explicit reference to the director's previous film.) Each morning, Kubrick would empty the set and he and Sellers would go over the lines as written, then go off at different tangents until something clicked. When Kubrick found what he wanted, he filmed Sellers with three or more cameras – Sellers usually performed best on the first take with subsequent takes showing a dilution of energy and interest.

Kubrick's experience with Olivier, Ustinov and Laughton on *Spartacus* had taught him that strong actors could bring an extra dimension to a film if they were given the time and space to get their ideas out into the open. He could then pick and choose the best ideas for the film. So before shooting began, Kubrick asked the actors to learn their lines, forget them and then improvise them – the improvised words being the one they filmed. This was initially difficult for both veteran actor James Mason and 14-year-old Sue Lyon, who played Lolita.

Mason believed the script was fixed and that a performance came from an interpretation of the script. As soon as Lyon, a professional actress whom Kubrick had seen in an episode of *The Loretta Young Show*, understood, she 'made a considerable contribution to many of the scenes because she spoke the same language as the character she was playing' according to James Mason.[14] Again, Kubrick used music to get the cast into the right mood – something from *West Side Story* for Shelley Winters, a ballad for Sue Lyon and *Irma la Douce* for James Mason.

The film was shot at Elstree studios in England in 88 days for just over $2 million. It was then slightly edited to comply with the 'suggestions' of

LEFT
Still from 'Lolita' (1962)
The love triangle is perfectly explained when Humbert embraces Charlotte and looks at a photo of Lolita. This scene caused censorship problems because it implied that Humbert needed the image to make love to Charlotte.

ABOVE
Still from 'Lolita' (1962)
Lolita is secretly having an affair with the mysterious Clare Quilty. She is deceiving Humbert in the same way that Humbert deceived Charlotte.

PAGES 78/79
Still from 'Lolita' (1962)
Lolita seduces a nervous Humbert with lessons she learned at Camp Climax. The shadows suggest Humbert is trapped.

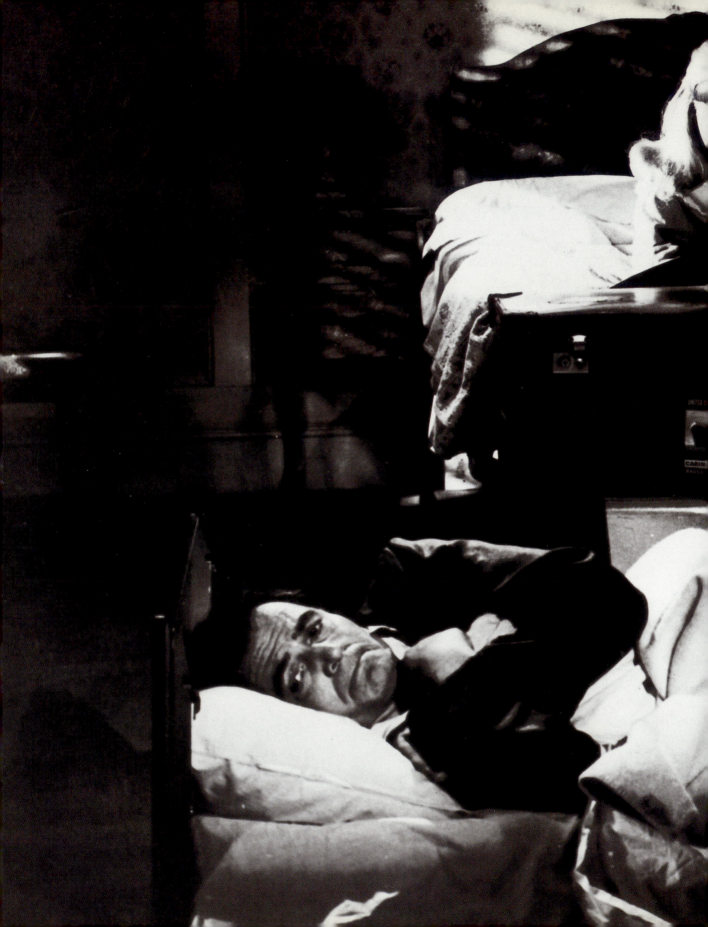

ABOVE
Still from 'Lolita' (1962)
Humbert is repulsed by the thought of sex with Charlotte.

RIGHT
Still from 'Lolita' (1962)
Charlotte reads Humbert's diaries and finds declarations of his love for Lolita.

the censoring bodies. Harris and Kubrick had been sensible enough to liaise with the censors throughout the production process to lessen any effect they might have. The film was released to mixed reviews and box-office receipts of $3.7 million on its opening run.

Like *Killer's Kiss* and *Spartacus*, *Lolita* is the story of two men fighting for the same woman. Although Lolita is the object of desire for both Humbert and Quilty, the film concentrates on Humbert's point of view. Kubrick shows a hypocritical society which indulges in wife-swapping and other sexual activities, so that Humbert seems quite reasonable in comparison.

At first urbane and witty, once Humbert is with Lolita he becomes insecure and by the end of the story he is a cold man full of self-disgust. Humbert recognises that Quilty is his dark half, a mass of sexual obsessions without inhibitions. At the end of the film, Humbert sees that he must destroy this vulgar version of himself so that Lolita is free to live the life she chooses. However, rather like *Spartacus*, Humbert's self-sacrifice rings a little false. This is because the intention of the novel was for Humbert to lust after Lolita and only discover he loved her at the end, when she is pregnant and less attractive. It was necessary for Harris and Kubrick to edit out the erotic element of Humbert's relationship with Lolita, so right from the beginning we feel that he loves her rather than just lusts after her – this self-revelation is missing in the film.

Harris and Kubrick had pulled it off. They had taken a high-profile, controversial literary novel and adapted it into a film with no interference from any studio and only minor interference from the censors. It had been made cheaply in England so that profits were maximised for everybody. Harris and Kubrick had even set up companies in Switzerland so that they could take advantage of low taxes on their profits and have financial security for the rest of their lives.

At the end of 1961, Kirk Douglas allowed the Harris-Kubrick Pictures Corporation to buy out their contract with Bryna. So by the end of 1962, Harris-Kubrick had effectively gained their richly deserved independence from the film community. After returning to New York and setting up their next film, Harris decided it was time for him to start a directing career and Kubrick decided it was time for him to resume producing again. Harris set up offices in Los Angeles while Kubrick contemplated thermonuclear war.

LEFT
Still from 'Lolita' (1962)
The balance of power between Humbert and Lolita is always in flux.

ABOVE
Still from 'Lolita' (1962)
Humbert decides to end the conflicting emotions inside him by shooting Clare Quilty.

PAGE 82
Sue Lyon
Photo by Stanley Kubrick. Kubrick took several photos of Sue Lyon to capture different moods and attitudes.

PAGE 83
Publicity still for 'Lolita' (1962)
Humbert Humbert attends to Lolita's needs.

PAGES 84/85
Publicity still for 'Lolita' (1962)
Lolita becomes the seducer.

"People can misinterpret almost anything so that it coincides with views they already hold. They take from art what they already believe, and I wonder how many people have ever had their views about anything important changed by a work of art?"

Stanley Kubrick [1]

ABOVE
Still from 'Dr Strangelove' (1964)
Major T. J. 'King' Kong (Slim Pickens) enjoys
some stimulating reading on his way to nuke
the Russians.

RIGHT
Still from 'Dr Strangelove' (1964)
The B-52 bomber flying low over Russia
to avoid radar detection.

The nuclear bombings of Hiroshima and Nagasaki that concluded World War
Two sent a shockwave of paranoia around the world. In the subsequent Cold
War between America and the Soviet Union there was a palpable threat of
thermonuclear annihilation – it was believed that if one side pressed the button
then the other side would automatically retaliate.

For several years Kubrick had read widely about the subject of nuclear strategy and had reached the conclusion that nobody really knew anything and
that the whole situation was absurd. This had occurred to Kubrick whilst he
was adapting *Red Alert* by Peter George (originally published as *Two Hours
to Doom* under the pseudonym Peter Bryant). At first he and Harris worked
with Peter George in their New York office, but after the story became a satire,
Kubrick asked Terry Southern, pioneer of New and gonzo Journalism, to
pen the black comedy now called *Dr Strangelove or: How I Learned to Stop
Worrying and Love the Bomb.*

Only the initial premise of George's novel was used for *Dr Strangelove* –
the rest is all Southern and Kubrick. When General Jack D. Ripper at Burpelson
Air Force Base orders a nuclear attack on the Soviets, the B-52s head for their tar-
gets. Alerted to this unauthorised attack, American President Merkin Muffley,
General Turgidson and the joint chiefs of staff meet in the War Room. Although
every effort is made to help the Russians destroy the US planes, a lone B-52
piloted by Major Kong manages to drop its bombs. Unfortunately, the Russians
have a Doomsday Machine that kills all human and animal life around the
world if they come under nuclear attack. The Americans' greatest scientific

mind, Dr Strangelove, suggests that they should live in the deepest mineshafts for 100 years and breed – say 10 women for every man. The men in the War Room think this is a good idea.

There are numerous sexual allusions in the words and images: the opening shot of the phallic coupling of the planes refuelling is accompanied by the song 'Try a Little Tenderness'; Jack D. Ripper, named after the 19th century sex murderer, refuses to give women his precious bodily fluids yet fondles his phallic guns and cigars; Buck Turgidson, his name meaning 'male' or 'swollen,' uses missile jargon in foreplay with his secretary, wanting her to "start her countdown" and so that she'll be ready for "blast-off"; both of President Merkin Muffley's names are references to female pudenda; a bomb on the B-52 has the words 'Dear John,' which is the start of a letter breaking off an affair; Major Kong rides one of the phallic bombs to its climax; and the final images show the beautiful nuclear mushrooms/phalluses accompanied by the song 'We'll Meet Again.'

This is perhaps the most pessimistic of Kubrick's movies which, like *Paths of Glory*, shows a male society losing control of the world. The films seem almost like mirrors. General Ripper/Mireau has gone a little mad and unleashed something his colleagues cannot stop. Each story takes place in three locations: the château/War Room; the trenches/Burpelson air base; and no man's land/the B-52. At the end, after failing to avert the crisis (three men shot/end of the world), the men return to their normal routine none the wiser. In *Dr Strangelove*, that means that the Russian Ambassador continues spying and General Turgidson

Still from 'Dr Strangelove' (1964)
General Jack D. Ripper (Sterling Hayden) tells
Group Captain Lionel Mandrake (Peter Sellers)
about keeping hold of his "precious bodily
fluids."

Still from 'Dr Strangelove' (1964)
Major 'Buck' Turgidson (George C. Scott) was a caricature of General Curtis LeMay, the warloving head of US Strategic Air Command in the 1950s who once suggested that Vietnam be bombed "back into the Stone Age."

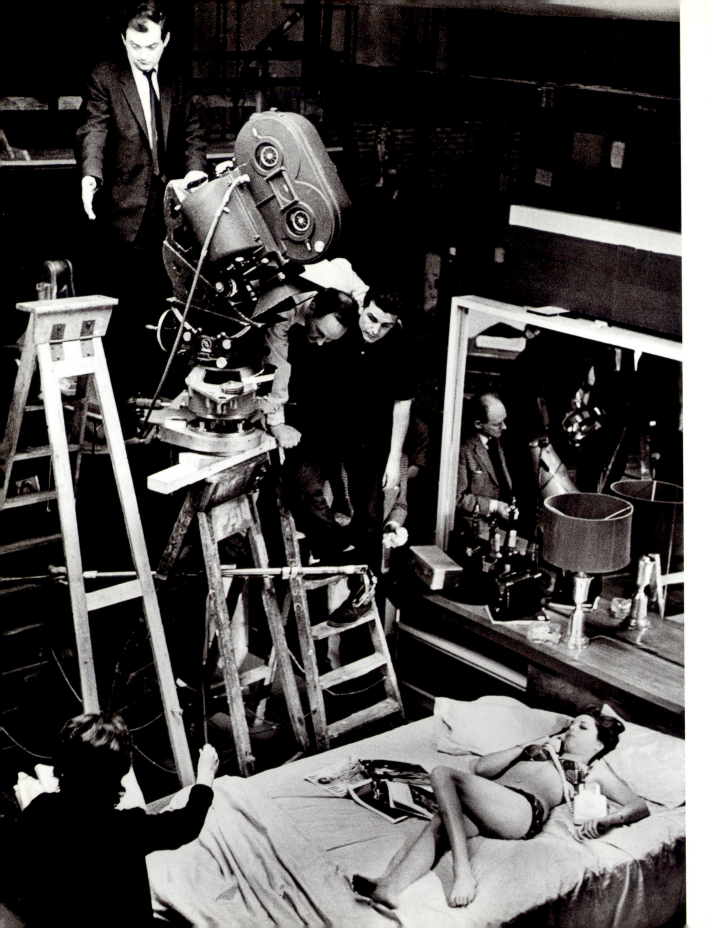

continues worrying about the mineshaft gap between them and the Soviets. Man may change the world around him, but man himself does not change.

Kubrick again filmed in England because it was cheap – this time at Shepperton Studios – and his family moved into a house in London for the duration of the production. Columbia, who were financing the film, were convinced that Peter Sellers was the reason *Lolita* had been a success so they insisted that Sellers be cast in the film and play multiple roles: Jack D. Ripper's confidante Lionel Mandrake, President Merkin Muffley and Dr Strangelove.

Dr Strangelove's strangled accent was based on Weegee, the famous German-born crime photographer of the 1950s whose name was given to him by the New York police due to his uncanny ability to show up at murder scenes before they did (i. e. as though he owned a Ouija board). Weegee was one of Kubrick's idols and he was invited onto the set to take stills. Sellers heard him talking and adopted his strange German accent.

The technical difficulties that had plagued *Killer's Kiss* were now solved thanks to advances in technology. Elaine Dundy reported that: 'The lighting – which incidentally Kubrick does himself – is simpler, what they call "natural lighting," i.e. coming only from what would seem to be the real sources of light in the situation instead of the complicated series of arc lamps hung from above that give most interior shots in films their unnatural quality. And no boom mikes. The actors often wear tiny concealed mikes on their persons.'[15] One of the prerequisites for Ken Adam's enormous War Room set was that the lighting would be real so that Kubrick could place his camera anywhere.

A custard pie fight in the War Room was filmed for a week but Kubrick cut it because he thought it was too farcical and consequently did not fit the dark satire of the rest of the film. At one point, President Muffley takes a pie in the face and falls down, prompting Turgidson to cry, "Gentlemen! Our gallant young president has just been struck down in his prime!" It was purely coincidental that President Kennedy was assassinated in Dallas on the day of the press launch, which was cancelled out of respect. This also necessitated a line change. Major Kong's comment about the survival kit ("A fella could have a pretty good weekend in Vegas with all that stuff") originally referred to Dallas instead of Las Vegas, but was overdubbed after the assassination.

Filming stopped in April 1963 after 15 weeks and then Kubrick spent eight months editing the footage together. The finished film was damn near perfect and earned $5 million in America, although it only cost $2 million to make. In his review for *The New York Review of Books* ('Out of This World,' 6 February 1970), Robert Brustein called *Dr Strangelove* a Juvenalian satire that 'releases, through comic poetry, those feelings of impotence and frustration that are consuming us all…'

It is the only Kubrick film not to have a central character who must choose between light and dark – the only shadows in this film are the shadows of ash on the walls of bomb sites.

ABOVE
Still from 'Dr Strangelove' (1964)
Major 'Buck' Turgidson. Would you trust this man's finger on the nuclear button?

OPPOSITE
On the set of 'Dr Strangelove' (1964)
Kubrick lining up a stand-in for Tracey Reed's scene with George C. Scott.

On the set of 'Dr Strangelove' (1964)
Kubrick deep in concentration during
preparations for the attack on Burpelson
Air Force Base.

On the set of 'Dr Strangelove' (1964)
An assistant holds Kubrick steady so he can
film with a hand-held camera.

On the set of 'Dr Strangelove' (1964)
Kubrick tells the soldiers where to shoot.

Still from 'Dr Strangelove' (1964)
The attack on Burpelson Air Force Base was actually an attack on Shepperton studios.

ABOVE
On the set of 'Dr Strangelove' (1964)
At this stage of his career, Kubrick was in
complete control of his set.

RIGHT
On the set of 'Dr Strangelove' (1964)
Kubrick uses his Tewe viewfinder to line up
a shot with Sterling Hayden and Peter Sellers.

*"Actors are essentially emotion-producing
instruments, and some are always tuned and
ready while others will reach a fantastic pitch
on one take and never equal it again, no matter
how hard they try."*

Stanley Kubrick[5]

94

ABOVE
On the set of 'Dr Strangelove' (1964)
Kubrick laughs.

LEFT
On the set of 'Dr Strangelove' (1964)
Peter Sellers (right) once said that Kubrick was a God. They had a great deal of respect for one another and shared an interest in photography.

"He's so self-effacing and apologetic it's impossible to be offended by him."

George C. Scott

On the set of 'Dr Strangelove' (1964)
Peter Sellers originally played President Muffley
upbeat. The crew laughed so much that a day's
shooting was lost. Kubrick decided that Muffley
should be the one sane man in the War Room.

Still from 'Dr Strangelove' (1964)
Peter Sellers played the mad Dr Strangelove
with an accent borrowed from the famous crime
photographer Weegee (aka Arthur Fellig) who
took stills on the set.

TOP **On the set of 'Dr Strangelove' (1964)**
The crew are ready to let the cast get their
just desserts.

MIDDLE **Still from 'Dr Strangelove' (1964)**
Kubrick deleted the pie fight because he thought
it was too farcical.

LEFT BOTTOM
On the set of 'Dr Strangelove' (1964)
George C. Scott reported that they threw one
thousand pies a day for a week. It was a lot of
fun but very, very messy.

ABOVE
Still from 'Dr Strangelove' (1964)
In the original ending Major 'Buck' Turgidson
announced that Dr Strangelove was the new
leader of the Western world after the President's
mind had snapped.

ABOVE
Still from 'Dr Strangelove' (1964)
President Muffley (Peter Sellers) decides to do
some reconstruction work after the devastation
that has been wrought during the pie fight.

PAGE 100
On the set of 'Dr Strangelove' (1964)
The apocalyptic ending has Slim Pickens riding
a nuclear bomb. Pickens knew what he was
doing – he had competed on the rodeo circuit.

PAGE 101 **On the set of 'Dr Strangelove' (1964)**
Slim Pickens balances precariously on a nuclear
warhead. The men in the foreground are pulling
ropes so that he does not fall.

PAGES 102/103 **Still from 'Dr Strangelove' (1964)**
Major Kong rides the warhead down to oblivion.

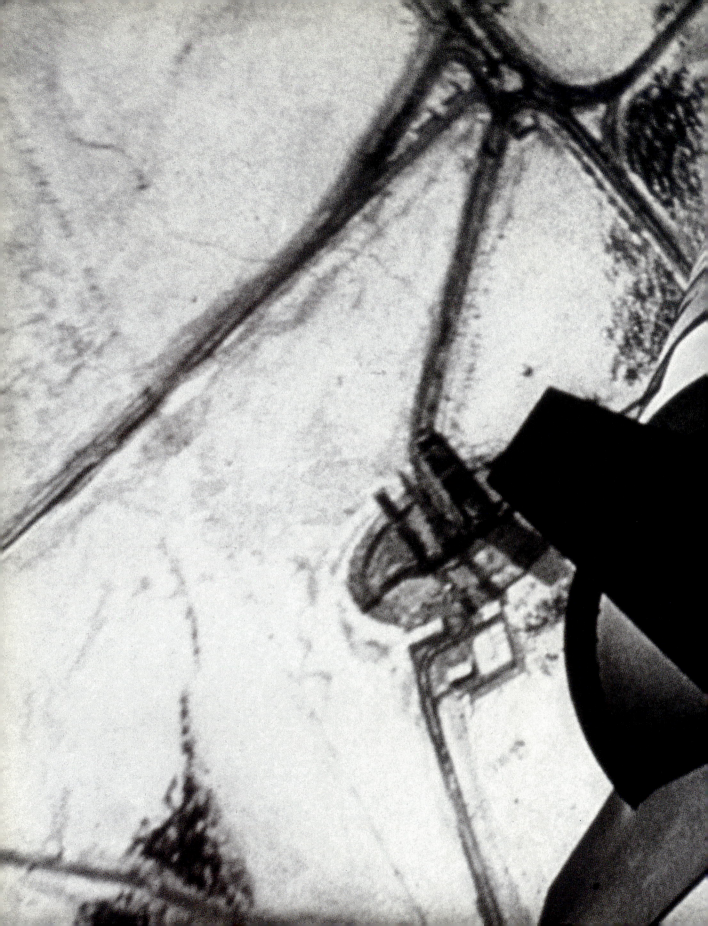

At one stage Kubrick had envisioned presenting *Dr Strangelove* as a documentary made by aliens. Although that idea was dropped, he was still interested in making a good science fiction film and wanted to find out who the good science fiction authors were. In February 1964, Arthur C. Clarke was recommended to him and two months later they met when Clarke visited New York to edit a book. Kubrick was impressed by Clarke's novel *Childhood's End*, which was about a superior race of alien beings who help mankind destroy their old selves, after which mankind is reborn one step up the evolutionary ladder. The film rights for the novel were taken but the idea of the novel stayed with Kubrick and Clarke as they fashioned their new film together. Clarke suggested that his 1948 short story 'The Sentinel' might be a suitable starting point – a tetrahedron is found on the Moon which alerts aliens to mankind's presence when it is penetrated. From May to Christmas 1964, Clarke wrote a novel of *2001: A Space Odyssey*, as it was later called, in the Chelsea Hotel (home to William S. Burroughs and many other beatnik authors) while Kubrick worked on the screenplay – they worked off each other's ideas to form a cohesive whole.

The story eventually coalesced into a visual poem about the evolution of man. Primordial apes gather for food and water, and sleep together. They are forced away from their watering hole by other apes so they find it difficult to survive. The monolith appears. One ape (Moonwatcher) finds out how to use bones as tools/weapons. They learn to hunt and eat the animals they once ate beside. The apes take back the watering hole from their rivals, and beat one of them to death.

In a future society we watch people eat and drink on spaceships. The monolith appears on the Moon. After this the Americans and Russians co-operate on a manned mission to Jupiter to discover the source of a signal to the monolith. On Discovery 1, Bowman and Poole eat, drink, play chess and draw. Their enemy is the supercomputer known as HAL who runs the ship, and who kills Poole and throws Bowman off his 'watering hole.' Bowman removes HAL's intelligence (essentially destroying the head, in the same way that Moonwatcher bashed in the head of the enemy ape). The monolith appears in space, and Bowman goes through a star gate, witnessing the wonders of the universe. In a familiar setting, an 18th-century room, he ages and transforms physically into a Star Child, then returns to Earth carrying his own environment with him.

Many other sequences were filmed, such as scenes of the home life of the astronauts, which would have been echoes of the domestic life of the apes, but little by little Kubrick cut them out. Interviews with experts on space, theology, biology, chemistry and astronomy were conducted for a ten-minute prologue. After the first screening for the MGM executives funding the film, Kubrick decided to delete the prologue. Dialogue explaining why the intelligent computer HAL had a nervous breakdown was deleted. The more cuts Kubrick made, the less dialogue remained. Kubrick said that "*Strangelove* was a film where much of its impact hinged on the dialogue, the mode of expression, the euphemisms employed. As a result, it's a picture that is largely destroyed in translation or dubbing. *2001*, on the other hand, is basically a visual, nonverbal experience. It avoids intellectual verbalisation and reaches the viewer's subconscious in a way that is essentially poetic and philosophic. The film thus becomes a subjective experience which hits the viewer at an inner level of consciousness, just as music does, or painting."[16] It also makes the film more ambiguous. "It has always seemed to

OPPOSITE TOP
Still from '2001: A Space Odyssey' (1968)
The planetary alignment signifies that something wonderful is about to happen.

OPPOSITE BOTTOM
Still from '2001: A Space Odyssey' (1968)
The apes eat, sleep and watch the night skies.

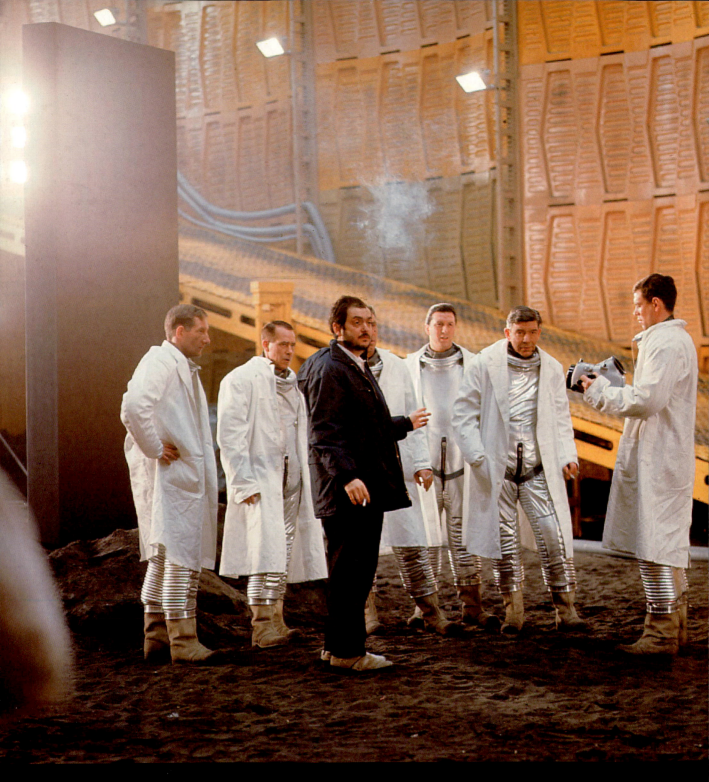

On the set of '2001: A Space Odyssey' (1968)
Stanley Kubrick and actors on the moon
excavation set have a cigarette break on the first
day of shooting, 29 December 1965.

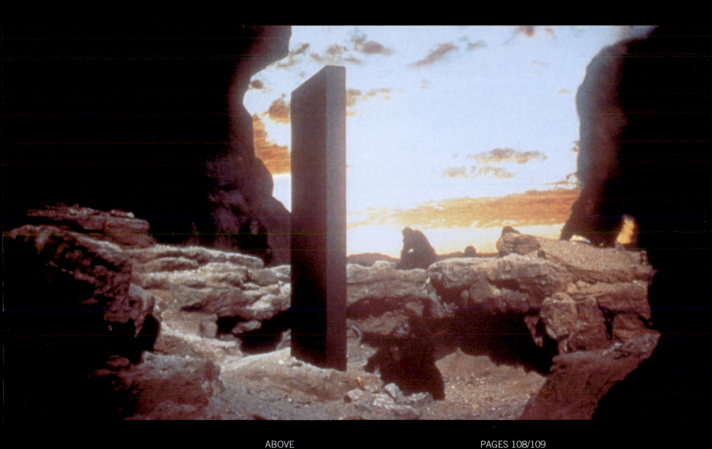

ABOVE
Still from '2001: A Space Odyssey' (1968)
The monolith appears in front of the apes and
seems to bestow intelligence upon them.

PAGES 108/109
Still from '2001: A Space Odyssey' (1968)
Moonwatcher (Daniel Richter) learns to use
a weapon – a reminder of the killer instinct
within us all.

Still from '2001: A Space Odyssey' (1968)
The Discovery with a space repair pod emerging from it.

me that really artistic, truthful ambiguity – if we can use such a paradoxical phrase – is the most perfect form of expression. Nobody likes to be told any-thing. Take Dostoyevsky. It's awfully difficult to say what he felt about any of his characters. I would say ambiguity is the end product of avoiding superficial, pat truths."

One of the 'pat truths' Kubrick may have been referring to was the original ending, where the Star Child returns to Earth and destroys the ring of nuclear bombs circling the planet. Although it is not made obvious, in the famous transi-tion when the ape throws his bone/weapon up into the air Kubrick cuts to a nuclear bomb in orbit. After the warning against nuclear Armageddon in *Dr Strangelove*, Kubrick did not want to be seen repeating himself in *2001*, so the ending was altered to the more ambiguous, and more satisfying, enigmatic stare of the Star Child. At the beginning and end of the movie, an evolutionary step is triggered by an outside force. Man continues to kill to protect his territory so that he can survive. The question is, will his evolution into a Star Child change anything or will man's nature remain the same? The film raises more questions than it answers.

The way Kubrick reduced *2001* to its most important elements was indicative of his emerging method of finding stories. Over the years, Kubrick had adapted so many books into films that he had realised that all he needed, as he later told Brian Aldiss, are "6 or 8 non-submersible units." A non-submersible unit is a story point that cannot be reduced. When these story points are linked together they form a narrative that will contain a balanced mix of all the themes, images and characters. As can be seen in *Dr Strangelove*, which has less than twenty scenes, and *Lolita*, these non-submersible units were already being refined by Kubrick.

Although the subtext of *2001* leaves room for interpretation, Kubrick's dedication to accuracy and detail, combined with his cinematic vision, meant that he researched every aspect of the plausible future so that it looked and felt real. The production, which moved from New York to the MGM Studios at Borehamwood, north London, in June 1965, had to keep up with the latest developments in the space race – Russian Andrei Leonov became the first man to walk in space on 18 March 1965, Ranger 9 photographed thousands of detailed pictures of the Moon for the first time, and American Ed White matched Leonov with his spacewalk on 3 June. The production team received cooperation from NASA and the companies making the spacecraft for the Moon landings, and visited them to find out how the spaceships would look and work.

However, the greatest challenge Kubrick faced was to find ways to depict things that had never been seen. To do this he assembled an incredible special effects team. When Clarke and Kubrick went to the New York World's Fair in 1964, Kubrick was so impressed by the NASA documentary *To the Moon and Beyond* that he asked the production company to do some preliminary work for him. Con Pederson and Douglas Trumbull eventually moved to London with the production, with the latter subsequently forging a glittering career on films like *Silent Running* (1971), *Close Encounters of the Third Kind* (1977) and *Blade Runner* (1982).

Kubrick had also liked the spawning of nebulae and star clusters in a National Film Board of Canada documentary called *Universe* (1959), so he hired the production team for *2001*. He rehired Wally Weevers, his special effects man from *Dr Strangelove*, who produced the best effects of his career, and he asked veteran Tom Howard, who had worked on optical effects for more than twenty years, to outdo the magic he'd created for *The Thief of Bagdad* (1940), *Blithe*

ABOVE
Still from '2001: A Space Odyssey' (1968)
The astronauts live in the centrifuge, from where they control the ship.

PAGE 114
On the set of '2001: A Space Odyssey' (1968)
Stanley Kubrick (left) discusses a shot inside the centrifugal set.

PAGE 115
On the set of '2001: A Space Odyssey' (1968)
The thirty-ton centrifugal set in motion. It generated so much heat that the hot air was sucked out by huge vents and cold air was pumped in.

On the set of '2001: A Space Odyssey' (1968)
The space repair pod was filmed separately and
then the other elements (the stars and Discovery)
were added afterwards.

Filming began on 29 December 1965 with the excavation of the monolith on the Moon. From 8 January 1966, it took a month to film the space station and moonbase sequences. Then the interiors of the Discovery 1 were filmed with actors Gary Lockwood (Poole) and Keir Dullea (Bowman) until the end of August. In a film full of stunning visuals, the engineering set piece was the control room of the Discovery for which Vickers Engineering built a centrifuge costing $750,000. Taller than a house, twenty feet wide and weighing thirty tons, the wheel rotated to give the effect of a centrifugal force within the Discovery. The outside of the wheel was plastered with floodlights, electrical equipment and projectors for the computer displays, which all combined to generate a suffocating heat. Consequently, enormous tubes sucked heat out and pumped air into the rotating set.

Kubrick watched the filming from inside a meshed cage, where video equipment fed images from inside the wheel. The disorientating effect of the wheel gave the viewer a sense of wonder about the marvellous tools that man could make. It was a stark contrast to the next sequence of principal photography. After a small team had photographed the Namibia desert for a couple of months early in 1967, the resulting images were projected onto a screen behind actors playing the apemen. (It was probably no accident that Discovery 1 looked like the bone used as both tool and weapon by the apes.)

Although the ape scenes were finished by the middle of 1967, the special effects teams continued with their complex and laborious filming until the end of 1967, often working to a twenty-four-hour schedule. In the end, more than 16,000 shots were taken to create the 205 special effects shots that would carry the visual thrust of the film. These were given an emotional dimension by a diverse range of music from Aram Khachaturyan, Richard Strauss and Johann Strauss. György Ligeti's angelic but menacing voice music accompanied the appearance of the monolith. Sound was very important to Kubrick, who used it to create an aural landscape. Space is silent, forbidding, mysterious, whilst inside Discovery we hear the warm, comforting, neutral tones of HAL 9000, the on-board computer. Kubrick tried actors Martin Balsam (too American) and Nigel Davenport (too British) before settling on Canadian Douglas Rain, who had narrated *Universe*.

After Kubrick previewed the film for MGM executives, he made many changes, and he made further cuts after the premiere – twenty minutes were removed and the intertitles were added to clarify time and place.

Many critics and filmgoers were perplexed by the film and it took a month before word-of-mouth generated a substantial audience. Although *2001* cost $10.5 million to make, it took $31 million worldwide by the end of 1972. It won the Oscar for Best Special Effects, the only Oscar Stanley Kubrick ever received. The film has since assumed mythical status and its power remains undiluted by the passing of time.

ABOVE
On the set of '2001: A Space Odyssey' (1968)
Stanley Kubrick and Gary Lockwood (right) share a relaxed moment. Anthony Frewin, who later became one of Kubrick's personal assistants, can be seen in the background.

PAGES 118/119
Still from '2001: A Space Odyssey' (1968)
The murderous gaze of HAL 9000, the supercomputer that runs the ship. Bowman (Keir Dullea) is reflected in the unblinking eye, showing HAL a picture he drew.

PAGES 120/121
Still from '2001: A Space Odyssey' (1968)
Bowman is mesmerised by his journey beyond the stars.

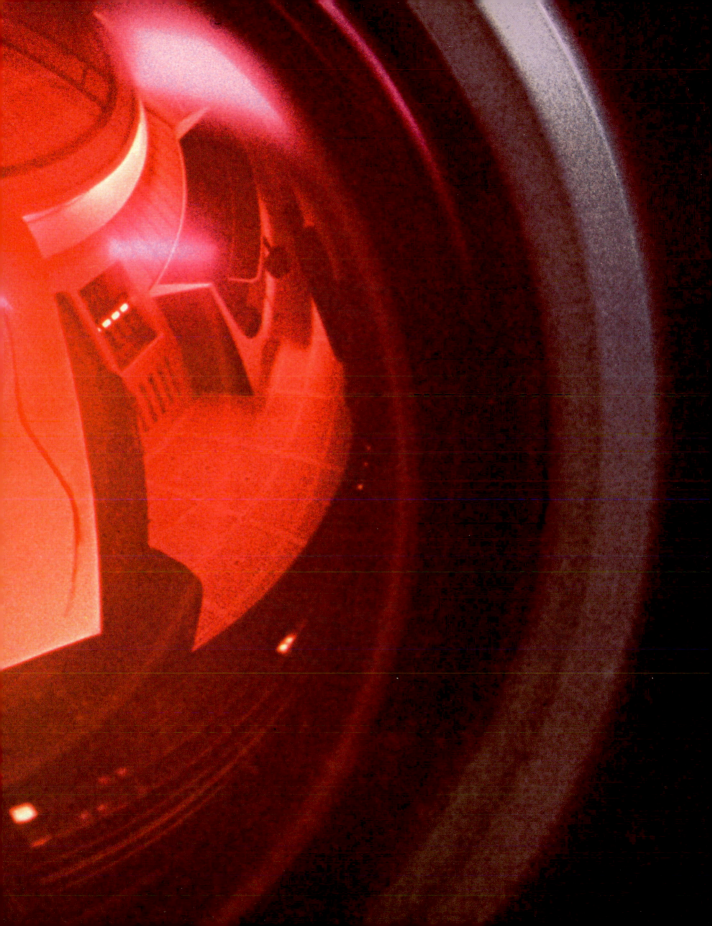

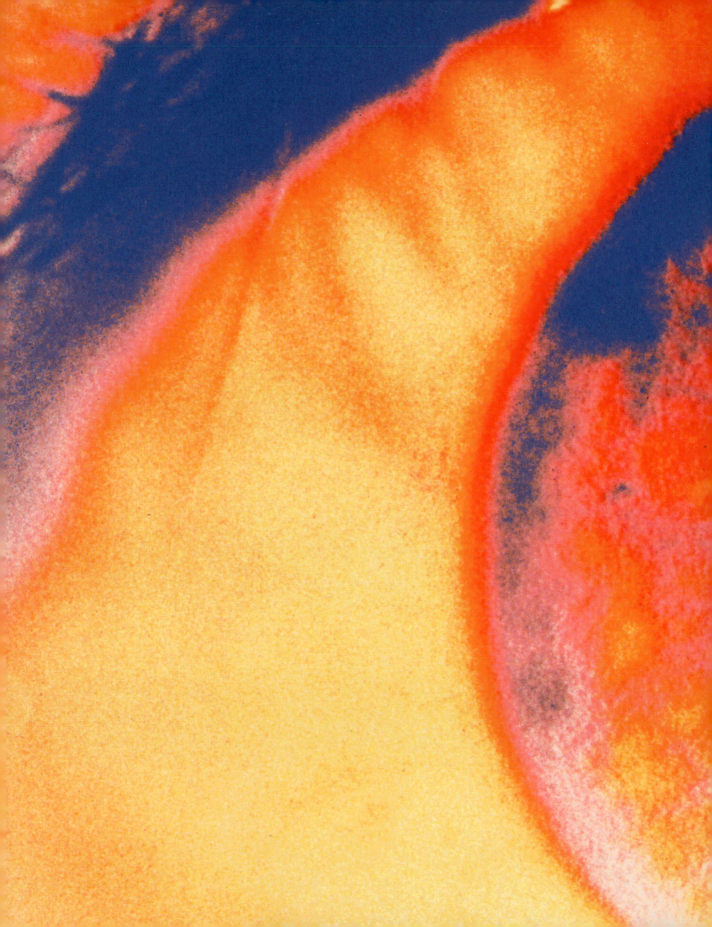

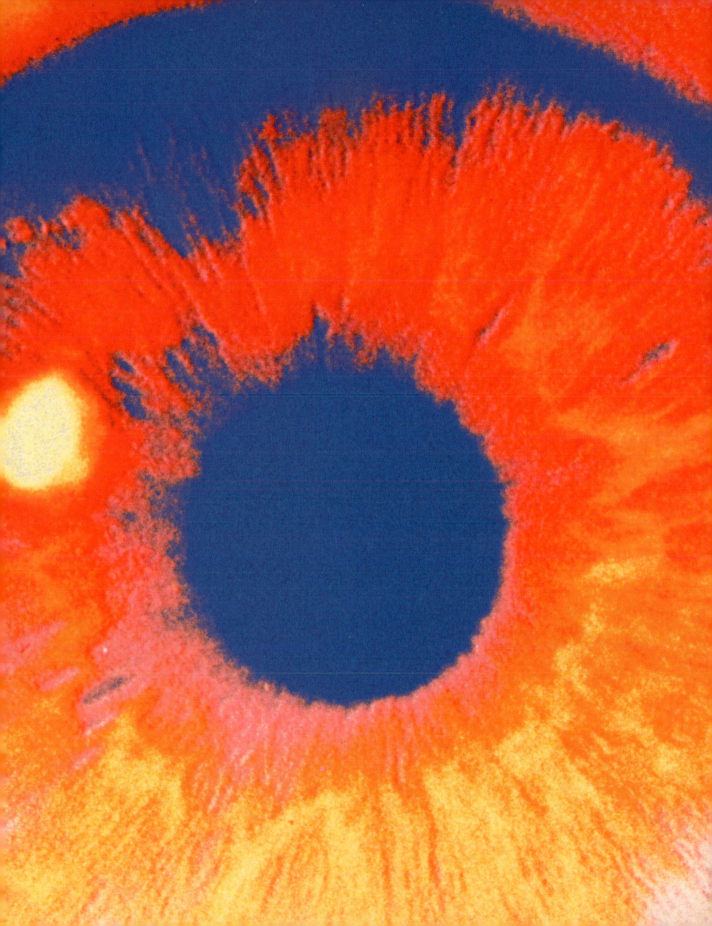

Still from '2001: A Space Odyssey' (1968)
The monolith appears at times of change for the human race. Here the aged Bowman sees the monolith just prior to his tranformation into the Star Child.

Kubrick had MGM eating out of his hand so in July 1968 he began work on his dream project, the life story of Napoleon.[17] He was fascinated by Napoleon because the latter caused his own self-destruction – human folly is, of course, a major Kubrick theme. Kubrick wrote a script and developed a film which required a country to hire out its armed forces. Detailed planning accounted for battle scenes with 35,000 people where 4,000 wore costumes and the rest wore throwaway overalls with designs painted on them. Researchers were sent all over Europe to find locations that matched the battle sites so that the strategic troop movements could be choreographed correctly. Napoleon had created modern Europe, and Kubrick thought the concerns of those times were contemporary – the responsibilities and abuses of power, the dynamics of social revolution, the relationship of the individual to the state, war, militarism and so on. Kubrick cast Jack Nicholson in the lead role after seeing him in *Easy Rider*

(1969) and, although the film was never made because of a change of ownership at MGM, Nicholson was so captivated by the subject that he hoped to film his own version of the Napoleon story.

Even though Kubrick had filmed *Lolita* and *Dr Strangelove* in England, he was still living in Greenwich Village with Christiane and the children when production on *2001* began. Fearful of the rising level of violence in New York, Stanley and Christiane decided to move to a safer environment. They bought Abbots Mead near Borehamwood, which was near Shepperton, Elstree and Pinewood Studios. Christiane continued painting, which was to become her second career, and the children enjoyed growing up in the English country-side. However, the violence they were escaping formed the central theme of Kubrick's next film.

Still from 'A Clockwork Orange' (1971)
The malevolence of Alex (Malcolm McDowell).
It is his nature to be evil.

ABOVE
Still from 'A Clockwork Orange' (1971)
Alex and his droogs (friends) prepare for some
ultra-violence.

PAGES 126/127
Still from 'A Clockwork Orange' (1971)
The droogs applaud the drunk's singing, just
before they beat him up. Note how Kubrick
uses noir lighting.

Still from 'A Clockwork Orange' (1971)
Alex goads Mr. Alexander (Patrick Magee)
just before he rapes the author's wife.

On the set of 'A Clockwork Orange' (1971)
Kubrick filming the above scene.

*"Aaron Stern, the former head of the MPAA
rating board in America, who is also a practising
psychiatrist, has suggested that Alex represents the
unconscious: man in his natural state. After he is
given the Ludovico 'cure' he has been 'civilised,'
and the sickness that follows may be viewed as
the neurosis imposed by society."*

Stanley Kubrick[1]

A Clockwork Orange, a 1962 novella written by Anthony Burgess, featured futuristic street gangs based on the Teddy Boys, Mods and Rockers who were fighting on the beaches of England during the late 1950s and early 1960s. On a trip to Leningrad, Burgess invented mnemonics so that he could speak Russian and from this derived a street language for the young teenagers called Nadsat – 'nadsat' is the Russian suffix for 'teen.' The thrust of the novel was simply that between the ages of ten and twenty-three youths indulge their desires for fornication, violence, stealing, drugs and other vices. The last chapter makes it clear that the central character, Alex, and his friends will grow up to become normal everyday members of society. It is as if their time of violence was a passing phase, a natural part of man's rites of passage.

When Kubrick first read the book – it had been given to him by Terry Southern when they were working on *Dr Strangelove* – he rejected it as a film project because he thought the Nadsat was too difficult to understand. Ironically, when Kubrick decided to adapt the book for his first solo script credit, he followed the book very closely, often word-for-word. He had read the American edition, which was missing the last redemptive chapter (the editor did not think it fitted the tone of the rest of the book) and this was the version he filmed over the winter of 1970–71 for $2 million.

Whilst *2001* ends with the benevolent serene stare of the Star Child, *A Clockwork Orange* opens with the malevolent smirk of Alex. Alex and his three droogs/friends have a drink of moloko/milk before going out on the town. They beat up a drunk, rumble a rival gang who are raping a woman, steal a car, drive like maniacs, attack writer Frank Alexander and force him to watch as Alex rapes his wife – Alex kicks, beats and rapes whilst singing and dancing 'Singin' In The Rain.' This scene was based on a tragic incident during World War Two when Burgess' first wife was attacked by four American deserters, which caused her to miscarry. Her resulting depression led to a suicide attempt. Writing the book was Burgess' way of getting rid of all the hate.

When Alex returns home, he listens to Ludwig Van Beethoven's glorious *Ninth Symphony*, imagining war, explosions, vampires, hanging, death and destruction. As Kubrick told Philip Strick and Penelope Houston, "Alex makes no attempt to deceive himself or the audience as to his total corruption and wickedness. He is the very personification of evil. On the other hand, he has winning qualities: his total candour, his wit, his intelligence and his energy; these are attractive qualities and ones, I might add, which he shares with Richard III."[18]

The following night, Alex uses a giant phallus to kill a woman and is abandoned by his droogs, who leave him for the police. Alex is sent to prison and, after two years of his fourteen-year sentence, volunteers for the experimental Ludovico Treatment, which will quickly cure him of his antisocial urges and release him back into society. The chaplain warns, "When a man cannot choose, he is no longer a man." Alex is given a drug, bound to a chair, his eyes are clamped open and he is forced to watch films of violence and depravity whilst listening to Beethoven's *Ninth Symphony*. After two weeks, the mere thought of sex, violence and the *Ninth* throws Alex into convulsions.

Alex is publicly tested in front of the press and government minister, then released into the world. His parents disown him, old age pensioners assault him,

PAGES 130/131
On the set of 'A Clockwork Orange' (1971)
Cast and crew have fun whilst filming the horrendous rape scene. Adrienne Corri is being carried by Warren Clarke. Stanley Kubrick holds the camera.

PAGE 132
On the set of 'A Clockwork Orange' (1971)
Kubrick is amused by Malcolm McDowell (foreground).

PAGE 133
On the set of 'A Clockwork Orange' (1971)
A more contemplative moment for Kubrick.

PAGE 134
On the set of 'A Clockwork Orange' (1971)
Kubrick lines up a shot with a stand-in for Malcolm McDowell holding the giant phallus.

PAGE 135
Still from 'A Clockwork Orange' (1971)
The murder of the cat lady is implied rather than shown. Alex rams the giant phallus down into her face.

two policemen (his former droogs Georgie and Dim) beat him up and he stumbles into the house of the writer whose wife he had raped. The writer kidnaps Alex and forces him to listen to the glorious *Ninth*. Repulsed by the music he attempts suicide and throws himself out of the window.

Waking in hospital covered in plaster casts, Alex's gulliver/head is put right by the doctors and the Minister responsible for the Ludovico Treatment offers Alex an interesting job with a good salary if he plays ball with the press. Alex listens to Beethoven's *Ninth* and thinks of having sex with a woman – he was cured all right. He was free to be evil again. Without Alex making the final choice of joining society, as in the novel, Burgess thought that: "A vindication of free will had become an exaltation of the urge to sin." However, Kubrick thought that the book's message had remained intact: "It is necessary for man to have choice to be good or evil, even if he chooses evil. To deprive him of this choice is to make him something less than human – a clockwork orange."[19]

After the enormous success of *Easy Rider*, many more independent films were made and the big studios clamoured to sign up all the hot new directors. The new freedom to show previously censored sex and violence appealed to Kubrick and influenced his decision to film *A Clockwork Orange*. Mainstream films like *Midnight Cowboy* (1969, director John Schlesinger), *Straw Dogs* (1971, director Sam Peckinpah) and *The Devils* (1971, director Ken Russell) had been given the dreaded X certificate (this generally indicated the film was pornographic and had no artistic merit) but had gone on to make money and even win Oscars.

A Clockwork Orange proved too controversial for several British newspapers. There were copycat incidents of ultra-violence, where people said the film had made them do awful things. This of course was nonsense because every person has free will – which was the point of the film – but the press did their best to exploit the story. Kubrick tried to defend himself: "To try to fasten any responsibility on art as the cause of life seems to me to put the case the wrong way around. Art consists of reshaping life but it does not create life, nor cause life. Furthermore, to attribute powerful suggestive qualities to a film is at odds with the scientifically accepted view that, even after deep hypnosis, in a posthypnotic state, people cannot be made to do things which are at odds with their natures."[20] Kubrick's arguments had no effect so he decided to stop the film (and by extension himself) being blamed for something it/he did not do by preventing it from being shown in the UK. *A Clockwork Orange* was not available for public viewing in the UK from 1974 until 2000, after Kubrick's death.

Kubrick could only do this because he had negotiated an extraordinary contract with his new financiers, Warner Brothers. He had been given $2 million to make the film, could have complete control, including final cut, and could take home 40% of the profits. With such an incentive, Kubrick made sure that he maximised his return by creating a cinema database and only showing the film in cinemas where that type of film generated large grosses. It was a strategy that earned the film $40 million on a $2 million investment.

With his incredible record for profitable films, from that moment on Kubrick had complete control over everything he made.

ABOVE
On the set of 'A Clockwork Orange' (1971)
Kubrick films a scene using a wheelchair and
Patrick Magee can be seen in a wheelchair in
the foreground. Kubrick used wheelchairs as
symbols of impotency.

PAGES 138/139
Still from 'A Clockwork Orange' (1971)
Alex is paraded in front of an audience to prove
that he is cured of his sexual and violent urges.
Virtually every Kubrick film has a scene where
characters perform on a stage or in front of a
camera.

PAGES 140/141
On the set of 'A Clockwork Orange' (1971)
Kubrick shows that politicians perform to gain
media approval.

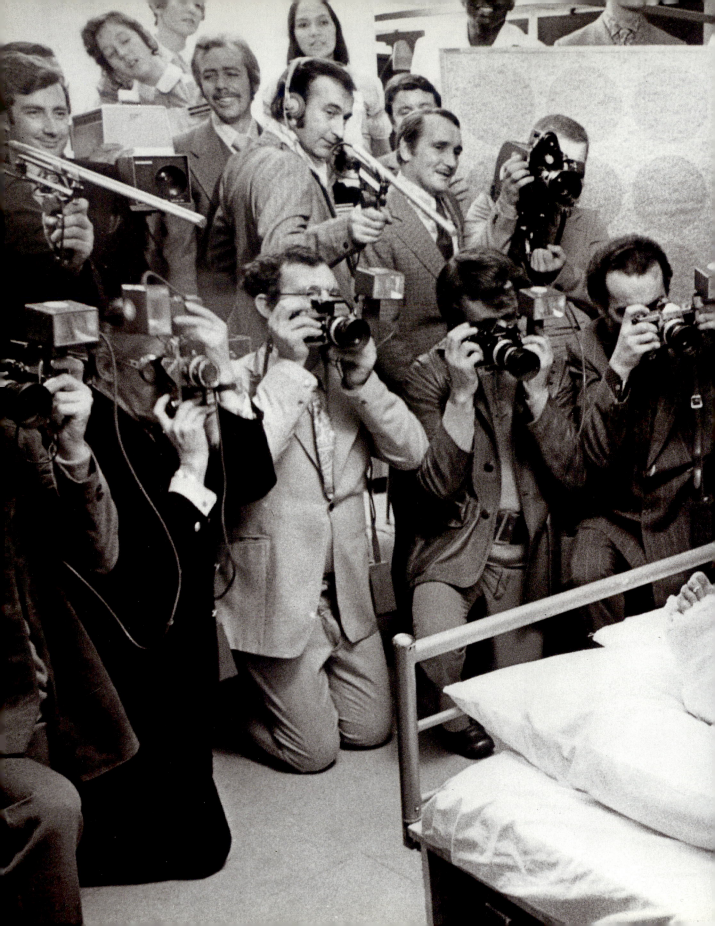

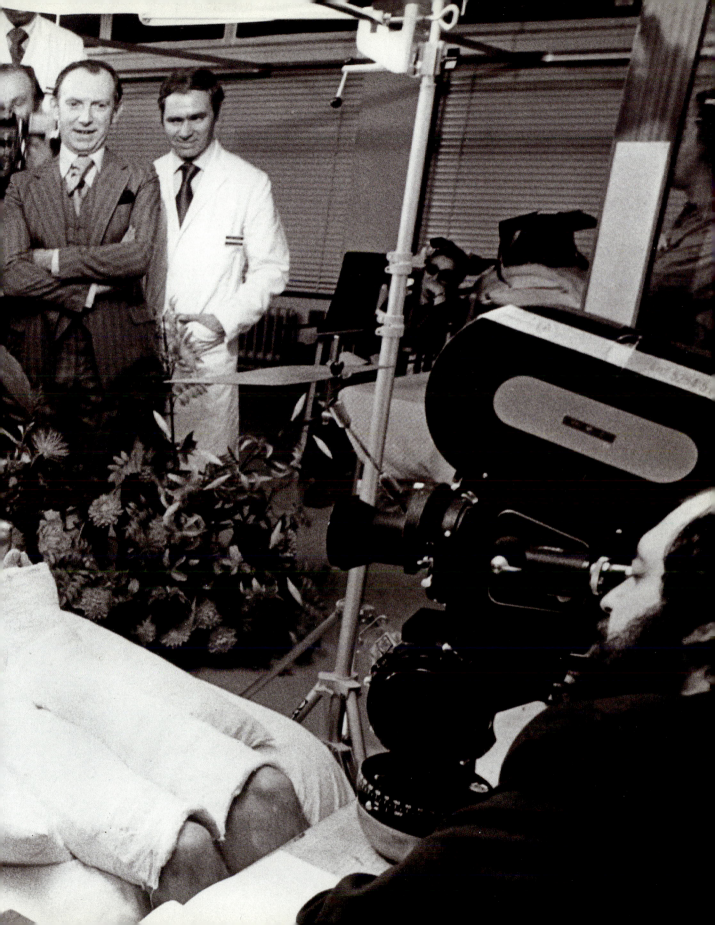

Still from 'A Clockwork Orange' (1971)
Alex is the narrator so we see everything from
his point of view, including his mental images.
The implication is that all the images, both real
and imagined, are part of Alex's fantasies.

Still from 'A Clockwork Orange' (1971)
When Alex is cured, the image he conjures echoes the rape of the woman shown to him during the Ludovico Treatment. Note that the audience is clapping (like the droogs applauded the drunk), showing their approval of his sexual display.

What Stanley Kubrick did next

Although Stanley Kubrick could ask for and receive budgets of millions of dollars for his films, at heart he was still an independent film-maker. He was passionate about every aspect of the production and felt it was his responsibility to do everything, as it had been on his early films. He told Robert Emmett Ginna, "I think you have to view the entire problem of putting the story you want to tell up there on that light square. It begins in the selection of the property; it continues through the creation of the right kind of financial and legal and contractual circumstances under which you make the film. It continues through the casting, the creation of the story, the sets, the costumes, the photography and the acting. And when the picture is shot, it's only partially finished. I think the cutting is just a continuation of directing a movie. I think the use of music effects, opticals and finally main titles are all part of telling the story. And I think the fragmentation of these jobs, by different people, is a very bad thing."[21]

Kubrick loved making movies – he did not take holidays because he considered himself to be playing, not working – and tried to surround himself with like-minded people, whether they had previous experience in the industry or not. He encouraged people to try new things and was a hard taskmaster – many people thought they did their best work trying to find out what would satisfy Kubrick's implacable intelligence. For the rest of his life, his exacting standards in all departments of the business and craft would make him legendary within the film-making community. Like Alfred Hitchcock, he would go to extraordinary lengths to present an accurate picture on the screen. Domino's apartment in *Eyes Wide Shut*, for example, was a studio set filled with the contents of a New York apartment that Kubrick had bought very cheaply. However, perhaps his greatest efforts towards authenticity went into *Barry Lyndon*, his most underrated and misunderstood film.

Kubrick failed to secure financing for *Napoleon*, but he still wanted to make an historical film and eventually chanced upon William Makepeace Thackeray's second novel, *The Memoirs of Barry Lyndon, Esq.* (1844). It is a long, picaresque story about the trials, tribulations and bad luck of Irishman Redmond Barry, told from his point of view. In 1960, Kubrick had written, perhaps thinking of *Lolita*: 'The perfect novel from which to make a movie is, I think, not the novel

On the set of 'Barry Lyndon' (1975)
Although Kubrick had a wealth of experienced
people around him, he always preferred to take
the shot himself.

Still from 'Barry Lyndon' (1975)
This is the shot Kubrick captured. He often used hand-held camerawork for fight scenes to give a sense of documentary realism and immediacy.

of action but, on the contrary, the novel which is mainly concerned with the inner life of its characters. It will give the adaptor an absolute compass bearing, as it were, on what a character is thinking or feeling at any given moment of the story.'[22] Interestingly, Kubrick dispensed with Redmond's narrative when adapting the script and inserted an ironic, cynical voice-over as a counterpoint to the feckless Irishman. Kubrick's legendary search for verisimilitude touched every aspect of the production. 18th-century costumes were bought and used as well as copied. The wigs were made from the hair of young Italian girls entering religious life. It was filmed entirely on location and no sets were built. Since Ireland still had many original 18th-century buildings, Kubrick moved the production there, travelling around the country. Some of the houses were still open to the public so Kubrick sometimes had to film between guided tours. Filming in Ireland stopped abruptly when Kubrick received threats from the IRA – he had been parading English soldiers in Ireland at a politically sensitive time in Ireland's history, with Bloody Sunday still fresh in the mind and killings a daily occurrence. The production moved to England overnight.

Kubrick painted with light and, like most artists, he liked to occasionally change his palette. For *Barry Lyndon*, he decided to photograph the 18th-century using its natural light – candlelight. It had never been done before but Kubrick obtained a lens made by NASA to use on the Moon and adapted a camera to carry it. This gave a soft grainy texture to the film which caused a problem for the camera operators. There was so little light going through the camera that they couldn't see the image to get the correct focus length. Kubrick simply attached a video camera to the film camera and used that for focusing as well as for instant replay on the different takes.

Kubrick was renowned for asking for many takes for some scenes. He told Michel Ciment, "…it's invariably because the actors don't know their lines, or don't know them well enough. An actor can only do one thing at a time, and when he has learned his lines only well enough to say them while he's thinking about them, he will always have trouble as soon as he has to work on the emotions of the scene or find camera marks. In a strong emotional scene, it is always best to be able to shoot in complete takes to allow the actor a continuity of emotion, and it is rare for most actors to reach their peak more than once or twice. There are, occasionally, scenes which benefit from extra takes, but even then, I'm not sure that the early takes aren't just glorified rehearsals with the added adrenaline of film running through the camera."[23]

The precision and attention to detail was important for this film because it is set in the age of the landscaped garden, when man attempted to control nature, to make it fit into calm patterns. Similarly, man tried to control his own nature by building an elaborate etiquette of behaviour. However, all he did was to mask his true nature. Using zoom lenses, which slowly revealed images recreated from the great paintings of the era (by Watteau, Hogarth, Gainsborough, Reynolds, Chardin and Stubbs), and classical music which lulls us into a sense of culture and nobility, Kubrick sculpts landscapes of civility that hide the barbarity lurking within the characters. Redmond Barry is the avatar whom we follow through these landscapes.

The story begins in 18th-century Ireland. Redmond Barry falls in love with his cousin Nora Brady, a flirt, and fights a duel over her, killing her fiancé, an

"Reactions to art are always different because they are always deeply personal."

Stanley Kubrick [5]

OPPOSITE TOP
Still from 'Barry Lyndon' (1975)
The film was set at a time when people tried to civilise the landscape.

OPPOSITE BOTTOM
Still from 'Barry Lyndon' (1975)
Barry talks to his stepson Lord Bullingdon (Dominic Savage) but right from the beginning Bullingdon knows that Barry married for the money. Lady Lyndon (Marisa Berenson) watches her husband with their son Brian.

PAGE 154
Publicity shot for 'Barry Lyndon' (1975)
Lady Lyndon is loved and protected by her son Lord Bullingdon.

PAGE 155 TOP
Still from 'Barry Lyndon' (1975)
The Chevalier (Patrick Magee) and Barry make their living playing at the game tables of Europe. Barry's idealistic love for his cousin has been replaced by a cynical desire for the same kind of wealth Captain Quin has.

PAGE 155 BOTTOM
Still from 'Barry Lyndon' (1975)
Bored with home life, Barry prefers to gamble and whore. The elegantly manicured world of the 18th century is merely a facade put up to hide the worse vices of humanity.

Still from 'Barry Lyndon' (1975)
Lord Bullingdon (Leon Vitali) causes Brian to interrupt a music recital. The ferocity of Barry's anger towards Bullingdon makes Barry an outcast from the society he was trying to buy himself into.

English soldier. He runs away to Dublin, joins the English army, has many adventures and eventually travels Europe with professional gambler, the Chevalier, swindling money out of the upper classes. The money is paid as promissory notes and Redmond duels with the Lords to force payment. The money is not enough to keep him in the style to which he is accustomed so he courts and marries a rich widow – Lady Lyndon.

Immediately after their marriage on 15 June 1773, it is made clear to Lady Lyndon that Barry is indifferent to her when she complains to Barry about his pipe smoke and he blows the smoke into her face. Barry is enchanted by all the things his new-found wealth can buy, so he gambles and fornicates without regard for his wife or her ten-year-old son, Lord Bullingdon, who knows that Barry is a mere opportunist. A son is born from the union, Brian, who grows up greatly loved by his father and is used by Lord Bullingdon to disrupt a formal musical recital in front of visiting dignitaries. Barry erupts with rage, attacks Bullingdon and has to be held back. This outburst turns Barry into an outcast from restrained society – his 'friends' make their excuses and turn down dinner and visiting invitations, believing Barry to be some sort of brute. These are the people he had been bribing so that he could obtain a title and improve his social standing. His debts begin to mount and, when Brian dies after falling off a horse, the parents are lost in despair – Barry finds solace in drink, Lady Lyndon becomes devoted to the church then tries to poison herself. Lord Bullingdon challenges Barry to a duel. When Bullingdon's pistol goes off accidentally, Barry fires into the ground. Instead of receiving satisfaction, Bullingdon continues and shoots Barry in the leg, which is amputated. Barry is playing cards

Still from 'Barry Lyndon' (1975)
In this Hogarthian image, Lord Bullingdon strides towards a drunken Barry to challenge him to a duel. As with the first duel, this is a matter of honour.

with his mother, when he receives an ultimatum from Bullingdon who offers Barry 500 guineas a year to get out of the country, otherwise his creditors will put him in jail. After several years in Ireland, Barry spends the rest of his life gambling in Europe, much as the Chevalier did.

It is a tragic story because after Redmond Barry's love is abused in Ireland, he does not allow himself the luxury of loving and abuses the love others give him. When he loves again – he lavishes his attention on Brian – his son dies and Barry returns to his cynical life a broken man. Kubrick skilfully weaves this tale without recourse to exposition and extensive dialogue scenes – like *2001*, many scenes are wordless and rely on the viewer to imprint their own thoughts and emotions onto the characters. Kubrick shows the audience and does not tell them. This is a consistent characteristic of his work, as he wrote in 1960: 'I think it essential if a man is good to know where he is bad and to show it, or if he is strong, to decide what the moments are in the story where he is weak and to show it. And I think that you must never try to explain how he got the way he is or why he did what he did.'[24]

After 170 cast and crew spent eight and a half months in vans travelling from one location to another, the film premiered on 18 December 1975 at a cost of $11 million. Although it was undoubtedly a masterpiece and won lots of awards, it failed to spark at the box office. Kubrick wrote that, 'The important thing in films is not so much to make successes as not to make failures, because each failure limits your future opportunities to make the films you want to make.'[25] Although he kept some of the props in his house and storage in the hope that *Napoleon* may get made, in his heart of hearts Kubrick must have realised that that dream was never to be.

"I think that the best plot is no apparent plot. I like a slow start, the start that gets under the audience's skin and involves them so that they can appreciate grace notes and soft tones and don't have to be pounded over the head with plot points and suspense hooks."

Stanley Kubrick[24]

Still from 'The Shining' (1980)
Jack (Jack Nicholson, right), Wendy (Shelley Duvall) and Danny Torrance (Danny Lloyd) travel to the Overlook Hotel, unaware of the horrors that await them.

Needing a hit, Kubrick read various books and then decided to do a horror movie based on Stephen King's best-selling haunted house novel *The Shining*. Kubrick decided not to read King's screenplay. This is understandable because King's work relies on readers empathising with the characters, whereas Kubrick liked to keep his characters at an emotional distance. Instead, Kubrick forged a relationship with novelist Diane Johnson and they concentrated on the dysfunctional Torrance family.

Kubrick's two previous movies featured dysfunctional families – Alex was a psychopathic 'outsider' who was disowned by parents who did not understand him, and Barry Lyndon was a father who doted on his son but ignored his wife and stepson to his cost. For *The Shining*, Kubrick showed how the duty of being a father and husband stopped Jack Torrance from writing and turned him into a potential killer.

The story is relatively simple. Writer Jack Torrance agrees to be the winter caretaker for the Overlook Hotel so that he can get some writing done. The manager tells him that in 1970 the caretaker, Delbert Grady, killed his wife and

two girls before taking his own life. "You can be rest assured it won't happen to me," Jack says, but we know that it will. When Jack arrives with his wife Wendy and son Danny, they are shown around the hotel before everybody leaves. Danny tells the hotel cook Dick Hallorann that he has bad visions involving two girls and the room 237. Dick also has ESP, which he calls "shining."

As winter sets in, the snow falls and the phone lines go down. When the family are cut off from the outside world things start to go wrong. Jack has writer's block and feels "as though I've been here before." Danny roves the corridors on his bike and sees two dead girls. When Danny screams and appears with a bruise around his neck, Wendy fears that Jack is hurting Danny again – Jack once dislocated Danny's arm when drunk, but Jack is on the wagon now. After Wendy confronts Jack about this, Jack wanders into the empty ballroom, and says: "I'd give my goddamn soul for a glass of beer." The barman – a ghost – serves Jack a drink.

Jack becomes more demented and, during a snowstorm, chases Danny through the maze at the back of the hotel, as Wendy confronts lots of ghosts

Still from 'The Shining' (1980)
Jack hopes that the solitude will break his
writer's block but he only becomes more
frustrated and impotent.

in the hotel. Wendy and Danny eventually escape in a snow-cat and Jack
freezes to death in the maze. A photo on the wall of the hotel, a 4th July
Ball in 1921, show Jack in the centre of the picture, smiling.

The film integrates two separate concepts: Danny's ESP and the haunted
house. When Dick Hallorann says, "When something happens it can leave
traces behind," he fails to mention that those traces can also affect the living.
In the case of Jack, he is angry and frustrated by his inability to work, to be
creative. The house accentuates this anger, uses Jack's repressed feelings
against him and gradually possesses him. Jack wants to drink and do violence. The house gives him the opportunity and excuse to carry out these
desires and hence turn against his family. Danny has ESP, and the house acts
on him through that power – it shows him the twins and asks him to join
them. Wendy is docile and ineffective, but she is the one who uses the
house most – she makes dinner, looks after the boiler, operates the radio.
She is the last to know what is going on and the last to see the horrors of
the house.

ABOVE
Still from 'The Shining' (1980)
When Jack says he'd sell his soul for a drink, suddenly the ballroom is full of people and the devilish bartender (Joe Turkel) is happy to serve.

PAGE 162
Still from 'The Shining' (1980)
Jack Torrance: "Heeeere's Johnny!"

PAGE 163
Still from 'The Shining' (1980)
Wendy recoils in terror when Jack becomes possessed by the hotel.

PAGES 164/165
Still from 'The Shining' (1980)
Cut off from the outside world, Wendy runs for her life.

"Realism is probably the best way to dramatise argument and ideas. Fantasy may deal best with themes which lie primarily in the unconscious."

Stanley Kubrick [1]

Dick says that he talked to his mother without speaking, so perhaps ESP is passed on from generation to generation. In the case of the Torrance family, it is from father to son, only both refuse to recognise the power. The father represses all acts of creativity and vision, so is unable to write. The son creates an imaginary friend, Tony, to account for his visions. This is probably Kubrick's bleakest examination of the dysfunctional family. The killer instinct in man has run amok.

The general perception of media people, who were more used to directors clamouring for space in their magazines, newspapers and TV programmes, was that Kubrick had become a recluse, and the observation has been made that Jack in the Overlook Hotel did bear a certain similarity to Kubrick in Childwickbury. Kubrick had bought Childwickbury in 1977, whilst preparing for filming on *The Shining*. A large, isolated house with woodland and lawns, it had extensive outbuildings for Kubrick's offices. He cooked and did the laundry whilst his wife painted and the children played. There was plenty of room for the cats and dogs, which he loved, although they sometimes got into mischief – one of his cats slept on his computer and urinated into it, necessitating the replacement of a circuit board. This was a far cry from the dysfunctional family in the Overlook Hotel.

The aerial shots of the Overlook Hotel were taken at the Timberline Lodge on Mount Hood in Oregon, with the frontage, maze and interiors built in Britain. To get an authentic look, thousands of photos were taken of hundreds of hotel rooms and then Kubrick picked the ones he wanted built. The Timberline Lodge asked that Kubrick did not use room 217 (as in the novel) because they were afraid nobody would want to stay in that room ever again. Kubrick changed the room number to the non-existent 237.

The camera prowls around the hotel thanks to Garrett Brown, inventor and operator of the Steadicam. He used the new camera to get smooth travelling shots in *Rocky* (1976) and *Marathon Man* (1976) but his improved version could be put lower to the ground and very close to walls. Brown shot most of the film, even still shots, because he could put the camera in positions other cameras could not go. The sets were also built to be connected, so that Brown could travel around the hotel in continuous shots.

Filming took place at Elstree Studios between May 1978 and April 1979, with the premiere in May 1980. Previously, Kubrick's films had opened small and built by word of mouth, but the large $10–15 million budget on *The Shining* meant that Warner Brothers had to do a media blitz to recover its money. The mostly negative reviews were offset by great box office – the opening weekend grossed $1 million, which was better than Warner Brothers' previous blockbusters *The Exorcist* (1973) and *Superman* (1978). It would gross $30.9 million in America by the end of the year, again justifying Warner Brothers' faith in Kubrick. It would be seven years before Kubrick had another film for them to release.

Still from 'The Shining' (1980)
Jack pursues Danny relentlessly through the maze.

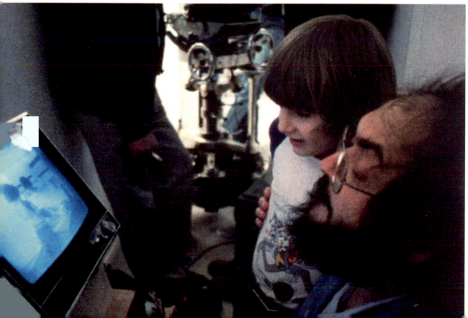

ABOVE
On the set of 'The Shining' (1980)
Garrett Brown (left), inventor and operator of
the Steadicam camera, gave the film its unique
look. Stanley Kubrick waits patiently in the
background, and his assistant Leon Vitali is
behind him.

LEFT
On the set of 'The Shining' (1980)
Kubrick watches a video playback of a scene
with Danny Lloyd.

OPPOSITE
On the set of 'The Shining' (1980)
Stanley Kubrick and Jack Nicholson.

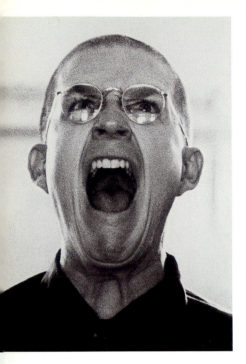

In 1980, Kubrick met Michael Herr through their mutual friend David Cornwell (a.k.a. novelist John le Carré). Herr was the author of *Dispatches*, a book of reportage about the Vietnam war, and had written Martin Sheen's narration for *Apocalypse Now* (1979, directed by Francis Ford Coppola). Kubrick and Herr were constantly on the phone in a period Herr described as a three-year phone call with interruptions. Then Kubrick found Gustav Hasford's Vietnam war novel *The Short-Timers*, a brutally honest, sometimes surreal story of grunts being trained as Marines and then sent to war. Like *A Clockwork Orange*, it was a short novel with its own specific jargon. Kubrick worked separately with Herr and Hasford on the script. Hasford, a Vietnam veteran, wrote to his friend Bob Bayer on 11 December 1982: 'Kubrick, by the way, makes me call him "Stanley." I can't stand it. The guy is a thoroughly charming and easy-going guy, a real good ole boy. He could fuck my sister, if I had one. (I used to have one, but I guess we must be divorced now.) We are working on creating a "more satisfying" ending for *Shorty* [Hasford's nickname for *The Short-Timers*]. "But Stanley," I said, "the Vietnam war was not bloody well satisfying." "Right," he said, "but they made you go to Vietnam, and people are going to have to pay to see this movie."'

The film follows the novel very closely in the first section. As part of their training at Parris Island, South Carolina, platoon 3092 are shouted at and insulted and hit and embarrassed and shamed and bullied by Gunnery Sergeant Hartman. Hartman was brought to life in an outstanding performance by Lee Ermey, who had submitted an amazing audition tape. As with Kubrick's three previous films, video auditions were organised by his assistant Leon Vitali – the adult Lord Bullingdon in *Barry Lyndon*. Ermey was a former Marines drill instructor in Vietnam, until a rocket exploded bedding shrapnel into his back and arm in 1969. With his sick pay, he bought a brothel in Okinawa, which he turned into a drinking club. Whilst in Manila under the G.I. Bill in 1976, he got a part in *Apocalypse Now*, which led to other film roles. Ermey wanted the part of the drill instructor but Kubrick said he wasn't vicious enough, so Ermey got the auditioning actors together and began humiliating them and swearing at them for 15 minutes. Kubrick hired him, had the tape transcribed, and used some of the dialogue in the finished film. When the shoot started, Ermey and the actors met for the first time on camera when he is shouting at them – Kubrick wanted to get authentic reactions from his fresh-faced young actors.

The platoon sleep with their rifles and give them female names. Joker does not believe in the Virgin Mary, so Hartman shouts at him to change his mind. Joker does not, so Hartman makes him Squad Leader and tells Joker to look after fatboy Pyle. Joker teaches Pyle about his rifle, lacing his shoes, making his bed, getting over obstacles, parading and Pyle does well. Then Hartman finds a jelly doughnut in Pyle's footlocker – from now on if Pyle fucks up the rest of the platoon pays for it. That night, the platoon puts soap in towels, holds Pyle down, and beats him. Joker beats him hardest of all. Hartman tells them that Charles Whitman, who killed 12 people at up to 400 yards, and Lee Harvey Oswald, who shot the President twice, learnt to shoot in the Marines. The Marines sing happy birthday to Jesus: "We keep Heaven packed with fresh souls – our present to Jesus." Pyle starts talking to his rifle. He is a marksman, he is becoming a killer. They graduate. On the last night, Joker has fire-

watch, and finds Pyle in the head (toilets) with a gun and live rounds. ("7.62 millimetre with full metal jacket.") Pyle: "I am in a world of shit." Pyle shoots Hartman dead, puts the rifle barrel in his mouth and pulls the trigger.

In Vietnam, Joker and his photographer friend Rafterman work for *Stars and Stripes*, the Army newspaper, where their job is to write propaganda not the truth. When the Tet holiday cease-fire is violated, US Army bases are attacked all over, dividing the country in half. Joker and Rafterman join the squad of his old bunk-buddy Cowboy. He says of the Vietnamese: "These people are the finest human beings…We're going to miss them." On patrol in bombed-out Hué city, the Lieutenant is killed by a booby trap and Cowboy is the new leader. They get lost. Eightball gets shot by a sniper. His body out in the open, the squad can do nothing as he is repeatedly shot. Doc Jay goes in to rescue Eightball and is shot. Cowboy is shot whilst radioing HQ. He dies. Animal Mother throws in smoke bombs to cover their advance across open ground. Joker finds the sniper, a young woman, but his rifle jams. She shoots at him. He is trapped behind a post. Rafterman shoots her. The squad look at her as she dies slowly, praying, asking to be shot. Joker shoots her. Rafterman is very pleased he shot the gook, and wants to make sure he gets the kill confirmed. Rafterman and Joker are now killers.

It is clear that this three-act film leads up to Joker's decision to kill, and debates whether or not he loses his humanity in the process. The purpose of the first third is to show how people are trained to be killers. This dehumanising process (the recruits are becoming weapons and are putting on 'full metal jackets' to protect themselves) results in dumb Private Pyle going mad and shooting himself because he cannot bear to live. The second third shows Private Joker as a journalist witnessing the bad things happening in Vietnam. Time and again, we are shown how the military command are failing to deal with the situation. Each individual soldier has to make the decision to kill. Joker talks the talk but cannot walk the walk – he has not seen combat.

The final third shows how people become killers. Joker finds out, first-hand, what it is like to watch people being killed. When it comes to combat, Joker fails – all that training was for nothing – because he still has intelligence and humanity. As an act of humanity, he kills the female sniper. His first kill comes out of compassion for his fellow human beings, not hatred. Joker's dual nature, as killer and compassionate human is evoked through his attire ('Born To Kill' on helmet, Peace badge on chest) and his words (in an interview Joker says he "wanted to see exotic Vietnam, the jewel of Southeast Asia. I wanted to meet interesting, stimulating people of an ancient culture, and kill them"). Joker's final words echo the last words of Pyle: "I am in a world of shit, yes, but I am alive, and I am not afraid." Joker can live with the fact that he is a killer.

Instead of travelling to some remote part of the world, Kubrick found he could film all the locations for Parris Island and Vietnam within 30 miles of his house. A square mile of marshes and old gasworks in Beckton substituted for Hué – the French architects had designed similar buildings in Hué. The buildings were due for demolition, so Anton Furst designed the set with the careful application of a wrecking ball. Filming began in August 1985 and ended later than expected, in September 1986, because Kubrick shut down the production for five months until Lee Ermey recovered after a near-fatal jeep accident off set.

When filming was complete, Kubrick added music by Abigail Mead – a pseudonym for his daughter Vivian Kubrick. The discordant music is very effective and created an unsettling, contemplative atmosphere. Abigail even turned Lee Ermey's Marine rap into a best-selling pop record that reached number two in the UK singles chart.

Released in June 1987, *Full Metal Jacket* was another hit for Kubrick – it cost $17 million and grossed $30 million in the first fifty days – but it was somewhat overshadowed by the earlier release of Oliver Stone's *Platoon*, which garnered all the plaudits. In *Dr Strangelove* and *Paths of Glory* it had been easy to see that the madness of war was due to the pride and arrogance of the generals, whereas *Full Metal Jacket* concentrated on the attempts of Private Joker to remain sane in a mad, uncontrolled environment. Kubrick's film steadfastly refused to push all the usual emotional buttons, as had other Vietnam movies released around that time, and left audiences a little shellshocked and bewildered.

Kubrick worked on several projects after the release of *Full Metal Jacket*. He built a science fiction story called *A.I. (Artificial Intelligence)*, based on Brian Aldiss' short story 'Supertoys Last All Summer Long,' but he postponed it in 1991 because there was no way to put the effects on the screen. He then worked on *Aryan Papers*,[26] based on Louis Begley's first novel *Wartime Lies* (1991), which was a World War Two story about a Jewish boy and his aunt trying to survive in Nazi-occupied Poland by passing as Aryan. A 100-day shoot was to begin in the summer of 1993 for a Christmas 1994 release but Kubrick decided the subject matter was too close to Steven Spielberg's *Schindler's List* (1993) and dropped it – perhaps he was still wary of how *Platoon* had taken media attention away from *Full Metal Jacket*.

Spielberg's other movie for 1993, *Jurassic Park*, gave Kubrick the confidence that the special effects he wanted for *A.I.* could soon be achieved using computer-generated imagery. He developed a *Pinocchio*-like story with Ian Watson about a robot boy wanting to become real so that his mother could love him. At the same time, he worked on the visual aspects of the film with Chris Baker. In 1995 Kubrick talked to Steven Spielberg about the possibility of Spielberg directing and Kubrick producing, but both men were too busy to take the idea any further so Kubrick held onto the film for a later date.[27] While he waited for the technology to improve, Kubrick decided to make a small, intimate film based on a book he read in the early 1970s, Arthur Schnitzler's 1926 German novella *Traumnovelle*, published in English as *Rhapsody: A Dream Novel*. Kubrick and Frederic Raphael turned it into a screenplay called *Eyes Wide Shut*.

"Vietnam was probably the first war that was run – certainly during the Kennedy era – as an advertising agency might run it. It was managed with cost-effective estimates and phoney statistics and kill-ratios and self-deceiving predictions about how victory was the light at the end of the tunnel."

Stanley Kubrick [32]

Still from 'Full Metal Jacket' (1987)
Animal Mother in killing mode. Perhaps this is what Private Pyle would have become if he had not cracked.

Since *Barry Lyndon*, the central characters of Kubrick's movies had been contemplative and isolated from the world. Their environments seemed to reflect their inner conflicts. And such is the case with *Eyes Wide Shut*.

Kubrick told Michel Ciment that the book was, "… a difficult book to describe – what good book isn't? It explores the sexual ambivalence of a happy marriage and tries to equate the importance of sexual dreams and might-have-beens with reality. All of Schnitzler's work is psychologically brilliant…"[28] The book is set in 1920s Vienna, and concerns the marriage crisis of Doctor Fridolin and his wife Albertine – the film follows the book quite closely although it was updated to contemporary New York. "The book opposes the real adventures of a husband and the fantasy adventures of his wife, and asks the question: is there a serious difference between dreaming a sexual adventure, and actually having one?"[29]

The film begins with attractive couple Alice and Bill Harford going to Victor Ziegler's party and each flirting with other guests. Bill saves the life of Mandy, who overdosed in Ziegler's bathroom, but cannot mention it because of doctor-patient confidentiality. The following night Bill and Alice smoke some pot and argue. Alice reveals that when they were on holiday she saw a Naval Officer in the same hotel and that her desire for him was so overwhelming that, if he had asked, she would have left Bill and their daughter to be with him. While Bill is reacting to this revelation, he is called out because a patient has died. As he consoles the daughter, Marion, she reveals that she loves him and is willing to give up her current life for him.

Bill walks absentmindedly through the New York streets, contemplating his wife's imagined infidelity. Wishing to revenge himself, he goes to a beautiful hooker's room. As they are about to kiss, his mobile phone rings – it is Alice. Bill leaves and walks into the Sonata Café, where his friend Nick Nightingale is a pianist in a jazz band. Nick tells him about a place where he plays blindfolded to an audience of naked women performing sexual acts. Bill gets a mask and costume, and uses the password 'Fidelio' to enter a large house. There he witnesses lewd acts between different and same sexes but does not take a part in them. Even though they are all masked, they seem to know one another. A woman warns Bill to go, but he is apprehended and unmasked before he does so. The woman says that she will take Bill's punishment, and Bill is allowed to leave.

The following day Bill retraces his footsteps, to investigate his adventure. A hotel clerk tells him that Nick left in a hurry, a bruise on his face, accompanied by two men. At the gate of the large house, Bill is handed a note saying he is to give up. The prostitute left after she tested HIV positive. Bill realises he is being followed and is scared. In the newspaper, he sees that Mandy – the girl he treated at Ziegler's – is in hospital. He visits but she has died. He believes she saved his life at the party and her life was taken instead.

Victor Ziegler summons Bill, and says, "Suppose I said it was all staged, fake, a charade, to scare the shit out of you, to keep you quiet." Ziegler says that Mandy was the woman who saved Bill, but that she died of an overdose. Returning home, Bill tells Alice about his desire for revenge through infidelity. They are grateful that they survived their adventures, whether real or imaginary. "One night is not the whole life," Alice says to Bill. "No dream is just a dream,"

ABOVE
Still from 'Eyes Wide Shut' (1999)
Although Alice Harford (Nicole Kidman) only appears in a few scenes, her thoughts and ideas propel her husband into an unsettled world of betrayal and doubt.

LEFT
Still from 'Eyes Wide Shut' (1999)
Alice and Bill are about to kiss, but Alice has her mind on other things.

Still from 'Eyes Wide Shut' (1999)
When Bill and Alice get high on dope and start talking, it becomes obvious that Bill's preconceptions about Alice are completely wrong.

Still from 'Eyes Wide Shut' (1999)
Victor Ziegler (Sydney Pollack) explains to Bill
what has been really happening.

he replies. The couple are now aware that they have a problem and can try to address it.

The film's remarkable cinematography and slow pacing is reminiscent of the work of Michelangelo Antonioni, which featured carefully composed figures in landscapes, gliding camera movements and psychologically tormented lovers. Also of note is Kubrick's use of primary colours, which carry symbolic significance. Red represents temptation and sex, as can be seen in the Sonata Café, the cabbie's shirt, the car that takes Bill to the big house which is decorated in red, the clothing of the orgy leader, the hooker's front doors and Ziegler's pool table. Yellow is the colour of betrayal, as can be seen at Ziegler's party, in Marion's apartment and in Bill and Alice's bedroom. Blue is the colour of danger and fear. When Bill imagines Alice and the Naval Officer making love, it is shown with a blue background, and significantly blue is often a primary colour when Bill talks to Alice in their bedroom. Finally, purple – a combination of red and blue – is the colour of the sheets when Bill reveals all to Alice.

Filming began in England on 4 November 1996 and, as usual, Kubrick rewrote scenes each day depending on the nuances of the rehearsals and performances. As well as Tom Cruise and Nicole Kidman, Harvey Keitel and Jennifer Jason Leigh were hired at the beginning of the shoot. However, Harvey Keitel left after six months and was replaced by film director Sydney Pollack (*Jeremiah Johnson* (1972), *Out of Africa* (1985)) who was so brilliant in Woody Allen's *Husbands and Wives* (1992). Kubrick wanted to reshoot Leigh's scene with Cruise. However, by this time, Leigh had already started in the lead role of David Cronenberg's *eXistenZ* (1999), so she was replaced by Swedish actress Marie Richardson. Tom Cruise flew back to England to redo his scene with Richardson in April and May of 1998. Principal photography ended in June 1998.

After Kubrick cut the film and had an enthusiastic preview with Warner Brothers, Cruise and Kidman, he told Julian Senior, his closest colleague at Warner Brothers' London office, that he thought *Eyes Wide Shut* was, "my best film ever." It was certainly his most emotionally mature work. The following day, Sunday, 7 March 1999, Kubrick died in his sleep from a massive heart attack. He was 70. Five days later he was buried near his favourite tree in Childwickbury Manor.

On the set of 'Eyes Wide Shut' (1999)
Stanley Kubrick between takes of the masked orgy.

On the set of 'Spartacus' (1960)
Kubrick is behind the camera commanding a
large cast and crew on location in Spain.

On the set of 'Barry Lyndon' (1975)
Stanley Kubrick has often been portrayed in a bad light by the press, who failed to understand his working methods. He strived to find the perfect shot and this took time and patience.

Filmography

Day of the Fight (1951)

Crew: *Director & Producer* Stanley Kubrick, *Writer* Robert Rein, *Music* Gerald Fried, *Editor* Julian Bergman, *Assistant Director* Alexander Singer, B&W, 16 minutes.

Cast: Walter Cartier, Douglas Edwards (Narrator), Vincent Cartier, Nate Fleischer.

Day of the Fight is a short documentary about a day in the life of boxer Walter Cartier. It premiered at the Paramount Theater, New York, on 26 April 1951.

Flying Padre (1951)

Crew: *Director & Writer & Cinematographer* Stanley Kubrick, *Producer* Burton Benjamin, *Music* Nathaniel Shilkret, *Editor* Isaac Kleinerman, *Sound* Harold R. Vivian, B&W, 8 minutes 30 seconds.

Cast: The Reverend Fred Stadtmueller, Bob Hite (Narrator).

Flying Padre is a short documentary about the life and work of a priest who has to fly to his different parishes.

Fear and Desire (1953)

Crew: *Director & Producer & Cinematographer & Editor* Stanley Kubrick, *Writers* Stanley Kubrick & Howard Sackler, *Associate Producer* Martin Perveler, *Music* Gerald Fried, *Art Director* Herbert Lebowitz, B&W, 68 minutes.

Cast: Frank Silvera (Mac), Paul Mazursky (Sidney), Kenneth Harp (Lt. Corby), Steve Coit (Fletcher), Virginia Leith (Girl), David Allen (Narrator).

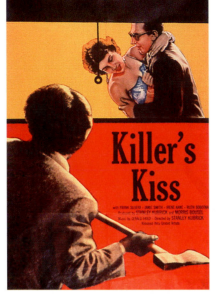

Fear and Desire is a war film about four soldiers who crash behind enemy lines and have to find their way home. The film premiered on 26 March 1953.

The Seafarers (1953)

Crew: *Director & Cinematographer & Editor & Sound* Stanley Kubrick, *Writer* Will Chasen,

Producer Lester Cooper, 30 minutes.

Cast: Dan Hollenbeck (Narrator).

The Seafarers is a full-colour documentary about the Seafarers International Union.

Killer's Kiss (1955)

Crew: *Director & Cinematographer & Editor* Stanley Kubrick, *Writers* Stanley Kubrick (story) & Howard Sackler (uncredited), *Producers* Morris Bousel & Stanley Kubrick, *Music* Gerald Fried, B&W, 67 minutes.

Cast: Frank Silvera (Vincent Rapallo), Jamie Smith (Davy Gordon), Irene Kane (Gloria Price), Jerry Jarret (Albert, the Fight Manager), Mike Dana (Gangster), Felice Orlandi (Gangster), Ralph Roberts (Gangster), Phil Stevenson (Gangster), Ruth Sobotka (Iris), Julius Adelman (Owner of Mannequin Factory).

Killer's Kiss is a noir melodrama about a boxer who wants to run away with a taxi dancer whose boss has sexual designs on her.

The Killing (1956)

Crew: *Director* Stanley Kubrick, *Writers* Stanley Kubrick & Jim Thompson (Dialogue), *Novel Clean Break* Lionel White, *Producer* James B. Harris, *Associate Producer* Alexander Singer, *Music* Gerald Fried, *Cinematographer* Lucien Ballard, *Editor* Betty Steinberg, *Art Director* Ruth Sobotka, B&W, 85 minutes.

Cast: Sterling Hayden (Johnny Clay), Coleen Gray (Fay), Vince Edwards (Val Cannon), Jay C. Flippen (Marvin Unger), Ted de Corsica (Randy Kennan),

Dr Strangelove: or How I Learned to Stop Worrying and Love the Bomb (1964)

Crew: *Director & Producer* Stanley Kubrick, *Writers* Stanley Kubrick & Terry Southern & Peter George, *Novel* Red Alert aka *Two Hours to Doom* Peter George, *Associate Producer* Victor Lyndon, *Executive Producer* Leon Minoff, *Music* Laurie Johnson, *Cinematographer* Gilbert Taylor, *Editor* Anthony Harvey, *Production Design* Ken Adam, *Technical Advisor* Captain John Crewdson, *Title Designer* Pablo Ferro, B&W, 93 minutes.

Cast: Peter Sellers (Group Captain Lionel Mandrake/President Merkin Muffley/Dr Strangelove), George C. Scott (General 'Buck' Turgidson), Sterling Hayden (General Jack D. Ripper), Keenan Wynn (Colonel 'Bat' Guano), Slim Pickens (Major T. J. 'King' Kong), Peter Bull (Ambassador de Sadesky).

Dr Strangelove is a comedy of terrors about an imminent nuclear holocaust.

2001: A Space Odyssey (1968)

Crew: *Director & Producer* Stanley Kubrick, *Writers* Stanley Kubrick & Arthur C. Clarke, *Story* 'The Sentinel' Arthur C. Clarke, *Music* Aram Khachaturyan (from 'Ballet Suite Gayaneh') & György Ligeti (from 'Atmospheres,' 'Lux Aeterna,' 'Adventures' and 'Requiem') & Richard Strauss (from 'Also Sprach Zarathustra') & Johann Strauss (from 'Blue Danube Waltz'), *Cinematographer* John Alcott, *Additional Photography* Geoffrey Unsworth, *Editor* Ray Lovejoy, *Production Design* Ernest Archer & Harry Lange & Anthony

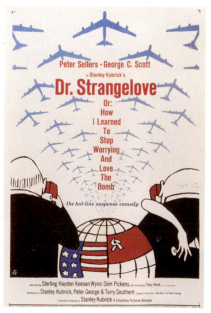

Marie Windsor (Sherry Peatty), Elisha Cook Jr. (George Peatty), Joe Sawyer (Mike O'Reilly), James Edwards (Parking Attendant), Timothy Carey (Nikki Arane), Kola Kwariani (Maurice Oboukhoff), Jay Adler (Leo Tito Vuolo), Joe Turkel (Tiny).
The Killing is a heist movie about a racetrack robbery.

Paths of Glory (1957)

Crew: *Director* Stanley Kubrick, *Writers* Stanley Kubrick & Jim Thompson & Calder Willingham, *Novel* Humphrey Cobb, *Producer* James B. Harris, *Music* Gerald Fried, *Cinematographer* George Krause, *Editor* Eva Kroll, *Art Director* Ludwig Reiber, *Military Advisor* Baron von Waldendels, B&W, 86 minutes.
Cast: Kirk Douglas (Colonel Dax), Ralph Meeker (Corporal Paris), Adolphe Menjou (Général Broulard), George Macready (Général Mireau), Wayne Morris (Lieutenant Roget), Richard Anderson (Major Saint-Auban), Timothy Carey (Private Férol), Joseph Turkel (Private Arnaud), Susanne Christian (German Singer), Bert Freed (Sergeant Boulanger).
Paths of Glory is a World War One film about three soldiers who are executed because of the mistakes of their superiors.

Spartacus (1960)

Crew: *Director* Stanley Kubrick, *Writers* Dalton Trumbo & Calder Willingham (uncredited), *Novel* Howard Fast, *Executive Producer* Kirk Douglas, *Producer* Edward Lewis, *Music* Alex North, *Cinematographers* Russell Metty & Clifford Stine (additional scenes), *Editor* Robert Lawrence, *Pro-*

---

duction Design Alexander Golitzen, *Title Designer* Saul Bass, *Second Unit Director* Yakima Canutt, *Historical & Technical Advisor* Vittorio Nino Novarese, Colour, USA première 184 minutes, then released at 161 minutes, 1991 restored version is 198 minutes.
Cast: Kirk Douglas (Spartacus), Laurence Olivier (Marcus Licinius Crassus), Jean Simmons (Varinia), Charles Laughton (Gracchus), Peter Ustinov (Lentulus Batiatus), John Gavin (Julius Caesar), Nina Foch (Helena Glabrus), John Ireland (Crixus), Herbert Lom (Tigranes), John Dall (Glabrus), Charles McGraw (Marcellus), Woody Strode (Draba), Tony Curtis (Antoninus), Anthony Hopkins (voice of Marcus Licinius Crassus in some scenes, 1991 restoration).
Spartacus is an historical epic about a Roman freedom fighter.

Lolita (1962)

Crew: *Director* Stanley Kubrick, *Writers* Vladimir Nabokov & Stanley Kubrick (uncredited), *Novel* Vladimir Nabokov, *Producer* James B. Harris, *Music* Nelson Riddle, *Lolita Theme* Bob Harris, *Orchestration* Gil Grau, *Cinematographer* Oswald Morris, *Editor* Anthony Harvey, *Art Director* William C. Andrews, B&W, 152 minutes.
Cast: James Mason (Humbert Humbert), Shelley Winters (Charlotte Haze), Sue Lyon (Lolita Haze), Peter Sellers (Clare Quilty), Garry Cockrell (Dick Schiller), Jerry Stovin (John Farlow), Diana Decker (Jean Farlow), Lois Maxwell (Nurse Lore).
Lolita is a comedy/drama about an older man who loves a very young girl.

Masters, *Special Photographic Effects Supervisors* Stanley Kubrick & Douglas Trumbull & Wally Veevers, Colour, 156 minutes for the Premiere, 139 minutes for General release. Germany 133 minutes.
Cast: Keir Dullea (David Bowman), Gary Lockwood (Frank Poole), William Sylvester (Dr Heywood R. Floyd), Daniel Richter (Moonwatcher), Leonard Rossiter (Smyslov), Margaret Tyzack (Elena), Robert Beatty (Dr Halvorsen), Sean Sullivan (Michaels), Douglas Rain (voice of HAL 9000), Ed Bishop (Lunar Shuttle Captain), Vivian Kubrick (Squirt), Anya & Katharina Kubrick (Painting Girls in deleted scenes).
2001: A Space Odyssey is a SF film/visual poem about the next step in mankind's evolution.

A Clockwork Orange *(1971)*
Crew: *Director & Writer & Producer* Stanley Kubrick, *Novel* Anthony Burgess, *Executive Producers* Si Litvinoff & Max L. Raab, *Associate Producer* Bernard Williams, *Music* Walter Carlos, *Cinematographer* John Alcott, *Editor* William Butler, *Production Design* John Barry, *Sculptures & Paintings* Christiane Kubrick, Colour, 137 minutes.
Cast: Malcolm McDowell (Alex DeLarge), Patrick Magee (Frank Alexander), Michael Bates (Chief Guard Barnes), Warren Clarke (Dim), John Clive (Stage Actor), Adrienne Corri (Mrs Alexander), Carl Duering (Dr Brodsky), Paul Farrell (Tramp), Clive Francis (Lodger), Michael Gover (Prison Governor), Miriam Karlin (Cat Lady), James Marcus (Georgie), Aubrey Morris (Deltoid), Godfrey Quigley (Prison Chaplain), Sheila Raynor (Mrs DeLarge, M), Madge Ryan (Dr Branum), John Savident (Conspirator Dolin), Anthony Sharp (Minister), Philip Stone (Mr DeLarge, P), Pauline

Taylor (Dr Taylor), Margaret Tyzack (Rubinstein), Steven Berkoff (Constable), Lindsay Campbell (Detective), Michael Tarn (Pete).
A Clockwork Orange is a black comedy which says that evil men have as much right to free will as good men.

Barry Lyndon *(1975)*
Crew: *Director & Writer & Producer* Stanley Kubrick, *Novel* William Makepeace Thackeray, *Executive Producer* Jan Harlan, *Associate Producer* Bernard Williams, *Music* The Chieftains &

Leonard Rosenman, *Cinematographer* John Alcott, *Editor* Tony Lawson, *Production Design* Ken Adam, *Historical Advisor* John Mollo, Colour, 184 minutes.
Cast: Ryan O'Neal (Barry Lyndon, born Redmond Barry), Marisa Berenson (Lady Lyndon), Patrick Magee (The Chevalier), Hardy Krüger (Captain Potzdorf), Steven Berkoff (Lord Ludd), Gay Hamilton (Nora), Marie Kean (Barry's Mother), Frank Middlemass (Sir Charles Lyndon), André Morell (Lord Wendover), Arthur O'Sullivan (Highwayman), Godfrey Quigley (Captain Grogan), Leonard Rossiter (Captain Quin), Philip Stone (Graham),

Being the adventures of a young man whose principal interests are rape, ultra-violence and Beethoven.

STANLEY KUBRICK'S CLOCKWORK ORANGE

A Stanley Kubrick Production "A CLOCKWORK ORANGE" Starring Malcolm McDowell · Patrick Magee · Adrienne Corri and Miriam Karlin · Screenplay by Stanley Kubrick · Based on the novel by Anthony Burgess · Produced and Directed by Stanley Kubrick · Executive Producers Max L. Raab and Si Litvinoff · WARNER BROS A WARNER COMMUNICATIONS COMPANY

A MASTERPIECE
OF MODERN HORROR

THE SHINING

A STANLEY KUBRICK FILM
JACK NICHOLSON SHELLEY DUVALL "THE SHINING"
SCATMAN CROTHERS DANNY LLOYD STEPHEN KING
STANLEY KUBRICK DIANE JOHNSON STANLEY KUBRICK
JAN HARLAN

& Ted Churchill, Colour, 119 and 146 minutes.
Cast: Jack Nicholson (Jack Torrance), Shelley Duvall (Wendy Torrance), Danny Lloyd (Danny Torrance), Scatman Crothers (Dick Halloran), Barry Nelson (Stuart Ullman), Philip Stone (Delbert Grady), Joe Turkel (Lloyd).
The Shining is a horror film about having writer's block in a haunted hotel.

Full Metal Jacket *(1987)*

Crew: *Director & Producer* Stanley Kubrick, *Writers* Gustav Hasford & Michael Herr & Stanley Kubrick, *Novel The Short Timers* Gustav Hasford, *Executive Producer* Jan Harlan, *Associate Producer* Michael Herr, *Co-Producer* Philip Hobbs, *Music* Vivian Kubrick (as Abigail Mead), *Cinematographer* Douglas Milsome, *Editor* Martin Hunter, *Production Design* Anton Furst, *Technical Advisor* R. Lee Ermey, Colour, 116 minutes.
Cast: Matthew Modine (Private Joker/Private J. T. Davis), Adam Baldwin (Animal Mother), Vincent D'Onofrio (Private Gomer Pyle/Private Leonard Lawrence), R. Lee Ermey (GySgt Hartman), Dorian Harewood (Eightball), Arliss Howard (Cowboy), Kevyn Major Howard (Rafterman), Ed O'Ross (Lt. Walter J. Tinoshky/Lt. Touchdown), John Terry (Lt. Lockhart), Kieron Jecchinis (Crazy Earl), Bruce Boa (Pogue Colonel), Kirk Taylor (Payback), Jon Stafford (Doc Jay), Peter Edmund (Private Snowball/Private Brown), Vivian Kubrick (uncredited News Camera Operator at Mass Grave).
Full Metal Jacket is a Vietnam War film about a soldier who comes to understand that he can do evil things and still live with himself.

Eyes Wide Shut *(1999)*

Crew: *Director & Executive Producer* Stanley Kubrick, *Writers* Stanley Kubrick & Frederic Raphael, *Novel Traumnovelle* Arthur Schnitzler, *Producer* Brian W. Cook, *Co-producer* Jan Harlan, *Original Music* Jocelyn Pook, *Additional Music* György Ligeti & Franz Liszt & Dmitri Shostakovich, *Cinematographer* Larry Smith, *Film Editor* Nigel Galt, *Production Design* Leslie Tomkins & Roy Walker, *Original Paintings* Christiane Kubrick & Katharina Kubrick (as Katharina Hobbs), Colour, 159 minutes.
Cast: Tom Cruise (Dr Bill Harford), Nicole Kidman (Alice Harford), Madison Eginton (Helena Harford), Marie Richardson (Marion Nathanson), Sydney Pollack (Victor Ziegler), Rade Serbedzija (Milich), Leslie Lowe (Ilona), Vinessa Shaw

CRUISE
KIDMAN
KUBRICK
EYES WIDE SHUT

(Domino), Todd Field (Nick Nightingale), Alan Cumming (Hotel Desk Clerk), Sky Dumont (Sandor Szavost), Louise J. Taylor (Gayle), Stewart Thorndike (Nuala), Julienne Davis (Amanda 'Mandy' Curran), Thomas Gibson (Carl), Leelee Sobieski (Milich's Daughter), Brian W. Cook (Tall Butler), Leon Vitali (Red Cloak), Fay Masterson (Sally).
Eyes Wide Shut is a film about fidelity in marriage.

Leon Vitali (Lord Bullingdon), David Morley (Brian Lyndon), Dominic Savage (Lord Bullingdon, younger), Michael Hordern (Narrator).
Barry Lyndon is an historical film about a man who searches for money and position and then loses all he possesses.

The Shining *(1980)*

Crew: *Director & Producer* Stanley Kubrick, *Writers* Stanley Kubrick & Diane Johnson, *Novel* Stephen King, *Executive Producer* Jan Harlan, *Music* Wendy Carlos & Rachel Elkind, *Additional Music* Béla Bartók & Hector Berlioz & György Ligeti & Krzysztof Penderecki, *Cinematographer* John Alcott, *Editor* Ray Lovejoy, *Production Design* Roy Walker, *Steadicam Operators* Garrett Brown

4 OSCARS
BARRY LYNDON
STANLEY KUBRICK
RYAN O'NEAL · MARISA BERENSON
mit PATRICK MAGEE·HARDY KRÜGER·DIANA KÖRNER·GAY HAMILTON
Herstellungsleitung JAN HARLAN

IN VIETNAM
THE WIND
DOESN'T BLOW
IT SUCKS

BORN TO KILL

Stanley Kubrick's
FULL METAL JACKET

WARNER BROS PRESENTS STANLEY KUBRICK'S FULL METAL JACKET
STARRING MATTHEW MODINE ADAM BALDWIN VINCENT D'ONOFRIO LEE ERMEY DORIAN HAREWOOD ARLISS HOWARD
KEVYN MAJOR HOWARD ED O'ROSS SCREENPLAY BY STANLEY KUBRICK MICHAEL HERR GUSTAV HASFORD
BASED ON THE NOVEL, THE SHORT TIMERS BY GUSTAV HASFORD CO-PRODUCER PHILIP HOBBS EXECUTIVE PRODUCER JAN HARLAN PRODUCED AND DIRECTED BY STANLEY KUBRICK

Bibliography

Articles by Kubrick
- 'Notes on Film.' *The Observer*, 4 December 1960
- 'Words and Movies.' *Sight and Sound*, Winter 1960/1961
- 'Ten Questions to Nine Directors.' *Sight and Sound*, Spring 1964
- 'Griffith and His Wings of Fortune.' *Speech at DGA Awards*, March 1997

Interviews with Stanley Kubrick
- Bean, Robin: 'How I Learned to Stop Worrying and Love the Cinema.' *Films & Filming*, June 1963
- Bernstein, Jeremy: 'Beyond the Stars.' *New Yorker*, 24 April 1965
- Bernstein, Jeremy: 'Profile: Stanley Kubrick.' *New Yorker*, 12 December 1966
- Cahill, Tim: 'The Rolling Stone Interview with Stanley Kubrick.' *Rolling Stone*, 27 August 1987
- Clines, Francis X.: 'Stanley Kubrick's Vietnam.' *New York Times*, 21 June 1987
- Duffy, Martha & Schickel, Richard: 'Kubrick's Grandest Gamble: Barry Lyndon.' *Time*, 15 December 1975
- Dundy, Elaine: 'Stanley Kubrick & Dr Strangelove.' *The Queen Magazine*, 13 March 1963
- Gelmis, Joseph: 'An Interview with Stanley Kubrick.' *The Film Director as Superstar*, Doubleday 1970
- Gilliatt, Penelope: 'Mankind on the Late, Late Show.' *The Observer*, 6 September 1987
- Ginna, Robert Emmett: 'The Odyssey Begins' (1959). *Entertainment Weekly*, 9 April 1999
- Hofsess, John: 'Mind's Eye: A Clockwork Orange.' *Take One*, May/June 1971
- Houston, Penelope: 'Kubrick Country.' *Saturday Review*, 25 December 1971
- Kohler, Charles: *Eye*, August 1968
- Nordern, Eric: 'Playboy Interview: Stanley Kubrick.' *Playboy*, September 1968
- Phillips, Gene D.: 'Stop the World: Stanley Kubrick.' *The Movie Makers: Artists in an Industry* 1973
- Phillips, Gene D. (ed.): *Stanley Kubrick: Interviews*. Mississippi 2001
- Rapf, Maurice: 'A Talk With Stanley Kubrick About 2001.' *Action*, January/February 1969
- Siskel, Gene: 'Kubrick's Creative Concern.' *Chicago Tribune*, 13 February 1972
- Siskel, Gene: 'Candidly Kubrick.' *Chicago Tribune*, 21 June 1987
- Southern, Terry: 'An Interview with Stanley Kubrick Director of Lolita.' Unpublished 1962
- Stang, Joanne: 'Stanley Kubrick.' *New York Times Magazine*, 12 October 1958
- Strick, Philip & Houston, Penelope: 'Modern Times: An Interview with Stanley Kubrick.' *Sight and Sound*, Spring 1972
- Young, Colin: 'The Hollywood War of Independence.' *Film Quarterly*, Spring 1959

Biographies, Memoirs, Analysis
- Agel, Jerome: *The Making Of Kubrick's 2001*. Signet 1970
- Baxter, John: *Stanley Kubrick, A Biography*. Harpercollins 1998
- Bizony, Piers: *2001: A Space Odyssey*. BFI 1997
- Bizony, Piers: *2001: Filming the Future*. Aurum Press 2000
- Bouineau, Jean-Marc: *Le Petit livre de Stanley Kubrick*. Spartorange 1991
- Chion, Michel: *Kubrick's Cinema Odyssey*. BFI 2001
- Ciment, Gilles (ed.): *Stanley Kubrick*. Dossiers Positif/ Rivages 1987
- Ciment, Gilles: *Kubrick*. Calmann-Lévy 1999
- Clarke, Arthur C.: *The Lost Worlds Of 2001*. Signet 1972
- Corliss, Richard: *Lolita*. BFI 1995
- Crone, Rainer & Graf Schaesberg, Petrus: *Stanley Kubrick: Still Moving Pictures, Fotografien 1945–1950*. Iccarus/Schnell+Steiner 1999
- De Vries, Daniel: *The Films of Stanley Kubrick*. William B. Eerdmans 1973
- Dumont, Jean Paul & Monod, Jean: *Le Foetus Astral*. Bourgeois 1970
- Duncan, Paul: *Stanley Kubrick*. Pocket Essentials 1999
- Falsetto, Mario (ed.): *Perspectives On Stanley Kubrick*. G. K. Hall 1996
- Falsetto, Mario: *Stanley Kubrick, A Narrative and Stylistic Analysis*. Praeger 2001
- Garcia Mainar, Luis M.: 'Narrative And Stylistic Patterns In the Films of Stanley Kubrick.' Boydell & Brewer 2000
- Geduld, Carolyn: *Filmguide to 2001: A Space Odyssey*. Indiana University Press 1973
- Ghezzi, Enrico (ed.): *Stanley Kubrick, Ladro di Sguardi, Fotografie di fotografie*. Bompiani 1994
- Giuliani, Pierre: *Stanley Kubrick*. Rivages 1990
- Herr, Michael: *Kubrick*. Pan Macmillan 2000
- Howard, James: *The Stanley Kubrick Companion*. Chrysalis 1999
- Hughes, David: *The Complete Kubrick*. Virgin 2000
- Jenkins, Greg: *Stanley Kubrick and the Art of Adaptation*. McFarland 1997
- Kagan, Norman: *The Cinema of Stanley Kubrick*. Roundhouse 2000
- Kubrick, Christiane: *Stanley Kubrick, A Life in Pictures*. Little, Brown 2002
- LoBrutto, Vincent: *Stanley Kubrick*. Faber & Faber 1998
- Nelson, Thomas Allen: *Kubrick: Inside a Film Artist's Maze*. Indiana 2000
- Phillips, Gene D.: *Stanley Kubrick, A Film Odyssey*. Popular Library 1975
- Raphael, Frederic: *Eyes Wide Open, 'A Memoir of Stanley Kubrick.'* Orion 1999
- Rasmussen, Randy: *Stanley Kubrick*. McFarland 2000
- Schwam, Stephanie (ed.): *The Making Of 2001: A Space Odyssey*. Modern Library 2000
- Walker, Alexander & Taylor, Sybil & Ruchti, Ulrich: *Stanley Kubrick, Director*. Weidenfeld 1999
- Wheat, Leonard F.: *Kubrick's 2001: A Triple Allegory*. Scarecrow Press 2000

Screenplays
- Kubrick, Stanley: *A Clockwork Orange*, Lorrimer 1972
- Kubrick, Stanley & Burgess, Anthony: *A Clockwork Orange*. Ballantine 1972
- Kubrick, Stanley & Herr, Michael & Hasford, Gustav: *Full Metal Jacket*. Knopf 1987
- Kubrick, Stanley, Raphael, Frederic, Schnitzler, Arthur & Davies, J.M.Q.: *Eyes Wide Shut*. Penguin 1999
- Nabokov, Vladimir: *Lolita, a Screenplay*. McGraw-Hill 1974

Documentaries
- Di Flaviano, Mauro & Greco, Federico & Landini, Stefano: *Stanley and Us*. (Italy) 2001
- Harlan, Jan: *Stanley Kubrick: A Life in Pictures*. (UK) 2001
- Joyce, Paul: *The Invisible Man*. (UK) 1997
- Joyce, Paul: *The Last Movie: Stanley Kubrick & Eyes Wide Shut*. (UK) 1999
- Kubrick, Vivian: *Making The Shining*. (UK) 1980

Bibliography
- Coyle, Wallace: *Stanley Kubrick, 'A Guide To References And Resources.'* G. K. Hall 1980

Websites
- www.kubrickfilms.com
- www.visual-memory.co.uk/amk/
- www.indelibleinc.com/kubrick/
- www.imdb.com

Notes

1. **Ciment, Michel:** *Kubrick*. Faber & Faber 2001
2. *Newsweek*. 26 May 1980
3. **Young, Colin:** 'The Hollywood War of Independence.' *Film Quarterly*, Spring 1959
4. **Ginna, Robert Emmett:** 'The Odyssey Begins' (1959). *Entertainment Weekly*, 9 April 1999
5. **Gelmis, Joseph:** 'An Interview with Stanley Kubrick.' *The Film Director as Superstar*, Doubleday 1970
6. **Phillips, Gene D. (Ed.):** *Stanley Kubrick: Interviews*. Mississippi 2001
7. **Duffy, Martha & Schickel, Richard:** 'Kubrick's Grandest Gamble: Barry Lyndon.' *Time*, 15 December 1975
8. **LoBrutto, Vincent:** *Stanley Kubrick*. Faber & Faber 1998
9. *New York Times*, 1 April 1953
10. **Colbert, Stanley L.:** 'Kubrick's Other Half.' *Creative Screenwriting*, July/August 1999
11. **James, Nick:** 'At Home With the Kubricks.' *Sight and Sound*, September 1999
12. See note 1
13. ibid.
14. **Butler, Ivan:** *The Making of Feature Films: A Guide*. Penguin 1971
15. **Dundy, Elaine:** 'Stanley Kubrick & Dr Strangelove.' *The Queen Magazine*, 13 March 1963
16. See note 5
17. The *Napoleon* script, research and production material is owned by Christiane Kubrick.
18. **Strick, Philip & Houston, Penelope:** 'Modern Times: An Interview with Stanley Kubrick.' *Sight and Sound*, Spring 1972
19. ibid.
20. ibid.
21. See note 4
22. **Kubrick, Stanley:** 'Words and Movies.' *Sight and Sound*, Winter 1960/1961
23. See note 1
24. **Kubrick, Stanley:** 'Notes on Film.' *The Observer*, 4 December 1960
25. ibid.
26. *Ayran Papers* is owned by Warner Brothers and available for film production.
27. After Kubrick died, Steven Spielberg made *A.I. (Artificial Intelligence)* with the approval of the Kubrick estate.
28. See note 1
29. ibid
30. **Kubrick, Stanley:** 'Griffith and His Wings of Fortune.' *Speech at 49th annual DGA Awards*, March 1997
31. **Cahill, Tim:** 'The Rolling Stone Interview with Stanley Kubrick.' *Rolling Stone*, 27 August 1987
32. **Gilliatt, Penelope:** 'Mankind on the Late, Late Show.' *The Observer*, 6 September 1987